Tribulation Saints

The Moment Truth Hits

A PRIMER ON HOW TO ENDURE TIL THE END

Michael Saunders & Randy Orris

Tribulation Saints

The Moment Truth Hits

How To Endure To The End

© 2011 Michael Saunders & Randy Orris

Love The Children Ministries

http://www.ltcm.wordpress.com

All rights reserved.

This book or parts thereof may not be reproduced in any form, stored in a retrieval system, or transmitted in any form by any means without prior written permission of the authors, except as provided by United States of America copyright law.

All scripture quotations are taken from The King James Version of the Bible (KJV), copyright © 1992 by Thomas Nelson, Inc. Used by permission.

Dedicated to all the Saints who will be overcomers.

Dedicated to all those that my Heavenly Father sent my way to help me write this book

Dedicated to my bride, who is patient while I spend hours at the computer writing.

Dedicated to Christ, who loves the unlovable.

Contents

- Foreword
- Introduction
- A Short Story
- Section I – In The Thick Of It
- How Could This Happen?
- Timothy DOD
- Little C – Big G
- No Other Gods
-
- Section II – OK, I Understand
- A Crash Course
- Now What?
- Let Me Tell You
- The Key Is In Your Hand
- Final Thoughts

Foreword

By Randy Orris

One of the most heart-searching and probing words that the Apostle Paul ever wrote are these which he had spoken to the Church at Galatia in the first century: "Am I therefore become your enemy, because I tell you the truth?" Galatians 6:14.

Michael Saunders is frankly one of the best friends you will ever have. He is telling the truth in an engaging and entertaining way. It's all here: the gripping Story of Sharon (which could be your own story someday) and the Study of the Second Coming of Christ (that clearly spells out the accurate events that are in our future).

You may not be particularly planning to go through the coming Great Tribulation. You may not want to go through it, and you may have been repeatedly assured by your favorite Bible teacher that if you have become a Christian you will never have to worry about going through any of it … but let's listen to what the Son of Man

Himself said about His Return and the Mark of the Beast. Understanding what Jesus said in Matthew 24 will open up The Book of the Revelation of Jesus Christ like you have probably never seen it before. Multitudes of true believers claim that they would never deny the Lord who bought them with His Blood. In one sense, we don't have to wait until those seven fateful prophetic years that a generation of Christians will someday face – untold multitudes are making that life or death decision right at this moment. As you read these words, there is a genuine born-again believer somewhere who has to make up his mind in the next 60 seconds.

The question is actually quite simple: "Will you at this moment choose to reject Jesus Christ as your Redeemer and Lord, and will you here and now deny Him? Or will you scream His name in agony as you draw your last breath – because you would rather die than deny?" The moments of time are slipping away quickly in front of your eyes. Choose.

The Christians in the early centuries had the same question put before them. "Kurious Caesar … or Kurious Christos?" Literally, "Will you chose Caesar as your

LORD, or will you choose Christ as your LORD?" The question was simple, but the answer that they gave, and the one that you give, has eternal consequences.

In this unforgettable book – TRIBULATION SAINTS – you are handed an Outline of those Events that you have been born to witness ... and to experience. This book may change your thinking ... and change your destiny.

In TRIBULATION SAINTS you will live through the prophetic events of this unavoidable future "Week" of Seven Years. You will be given practical tools to move forward through the accumulating darkness of those days. You will feel the pulse of today's church as it propels it's followers to tolerate sin and welcome a Global Religious Family worshiping a false god.. Deception has never been so deep.

You are being handed not only a Survival Guide, but also a very clear, compassionate warning of what exactly to look for, specifically what to avoid, and what to everlastingly embrace if you want to be spared from the impending judgments of the Living God.

Walk side by side with Mike Saunders as he shares his own powerful testimony of distinguishing between the wrath of Satan and the Wrath of God. There are few moments in life as breath-taking and stunning as "The Moment Truth Hits!"

The way out is the way in. IN CHRIST there is salvation, eternal life, and a life of continual discovery in the Knowledge of God. Knowledge that may well allow you to say "No!" when you will be asked to receive the invisible, organic tattoo that they will tell you that you can't live without.

They will be right about that statement. And they will be wrong about that statement.

The format of this end-times thriller is attractive, bringing us face to face with the greatest reality our generation will ever encounter! For those whose spirits are thirsty, and their hearts are hungry, to finally hear the sobering truth about what is coming, and will soon dramatically unfold before your very eyes – this book is your invitation to understand, and be prepared.

May the Holy Spirit use this Story and Study to awaken your heart, like it has mine. Truly what Jesus actually taught in "His Olivet Discourse" in Matthew 24 was not written for endless speculation, but rather, it is a concise and very startling time-line that every person on the Planet can readily grasp ... once they see it.

For those who are called to be watchmen, this book is your Field Manual; for those who just have to know how things will turn out in the end, this book is the Romance Story you've been looking for; for those who need a safe guide to walk them through the chaos and confusion that will cause millions to stumble in the dark, this book leads you to the truth of the Word, which is your Assurance Policy.

The pages of this book are crammed with vital information. Step by step, scripture by scripture, you will be equipped with the essentials of what is necessary to know "How To Endure To The End!" I promise you, this is a book will quickly become a companion to you, and one that you will have to share with everyone in your world. It is a book that will literally drive you to the Bible, to see what the Lord has revealed, because He loves you. And He doesn't want to live without you! With your Bible open, and the Spirit of Jesus unveiling your eyes page by page, you will be forever grateful for the day that this book come into your hands – and it's message was engraved upon your heart. I thank the Lord that my friend and fellow minister Michael Saunders has obeyed the Spirit's Voice in sending you this Last Days Manifesto. It could save your life, and the lives of those you love.

"Maranatha – Our Lord Comes!"

Randy L. Orris

Senior Pastor

Avondale, Arizona

Introduction

This is a unique book for many reasons. The first being that the greatest impact of this book will occur as it is read by many during perilous times. There are many who will not believe the things that I hear God telling me simply for one reason and one reason only; They don't think that God would ever allow them to suffer hardship. (More on that later) If you are one who feels that God will protect you from every danger as we approach the end times then this book is surely for you because the chances are good that you are reading this only after your favorite teacher or preacher, or your personal doctrine has been proven wrong. The rapture as you were taught has not taken place and seemingly, all hell is breaking loose.

Am I saying that I have all the answers and foresaw this? Not on your life! But I serve a God who loves His children enough to send watchmen to warn them. All I do is write what He tells me to write. I do not look for a bestseller from this. I do not look to craft a living from the proceeds of the great sales of this volume. As a matter of fact, just by the title I perceive that not many copies will be sold. However, by the title I also know that someone stumbling across this title who is in the middle of wondering what is going on will naturally gravitate towards this book. It may well be that almost every bookstore has closed it's doors and this is a copy that you were given. It may be so threadbare that the pages are falling out from passing through so many hands. But I am glad that God led you to it. I must assure you that in the midst of perilous times, God is there for you – the believer. And I simply must tell the story as I have heard it.

My previous book Walking Backwards was a treatise about bucking traditions that are contrary to the Word of God. After publishing that book I did not dream that God would have me to write about the End Times, but when He laid out the format in which I was to deliver the message I understood why He chose me. There are some who enjoy listening to theologians more learned than I. There are some who enjoy a format that is concise, like a textbook. I'm far more simple than that. I write like I speak, so dig in as I converse with you. I write for the poor in spirit.

This book begins with a short story about a young lady named Sharon. Maybe you can relate to her predicament. Maybe you are in a similar scenario, right now. I pray that our Father gives you the encouragement you need to carry on. I know He can and will for it is He that give the power 'To Endure Til The End'!

Mike

Bugout

Five days had passed since Sharon started her trek to the "bugout" location. Rick had given specific written instructions but made her promise that she would destroy them as soon as she had committed them to memory. Everything was mapped out based on walking 10 miles each day. She was thankful that she had only five days journey, as Rick had told her that some walked for weeks to the safety they sought.

At first she thought it strange that the location she was given on the crude map was not the real hideout, but only a pickup point where she would be met. The past days had been filled with second guessing. The enemy of her soul had practically perched on her shoulder whispering that she was wrong in her decision. Sharon was a determined young lady and stayed continually in thoughts and prayer, and that communion with her Father propelled her onward. Even before leaving she had moved out from her parents house.

Five days of wanting to turn around and go back to family that she had left behind. But she knew that was not a good decision, for they had all taken the mark. She knew from

Rick's teaching and the scriptures that their future was now secure. They would no longer have a portion in the Kingdom. She shuddered at the thought of being younger and having to take the mark simply because her parents would have required it.

Five days of living off the meager rations in her backpack and sipping water with care, hoping that the water lasted. Food was scarce and clean water just as hard to find. The filter bottle she had been given had only so many uses before she would have to start boiling water from whatever source she could find. She only could hope and pray that what was in her pack would sustain her. Memories of watching survival shows on the television years ago came back to her, and she laughed out loud at the thought of what she had in her little backpack.

There was no specialized titanium cook set, nor a host of freeze dried goodies to snack on. Her fire starter, should she dare to build a fire was an old butane lighter that she could only hope would last. She had become proficient in the art of doing with little. A true minimalist would have nothing on her, as the past few years of poverty had taught her well how to conserve.

The route had specific locations for her to stop at along the way. She was instructed to leave something to eat at each one. At first she thought that was a little much to ask of someone who scarcely had enough to eat, but as she had stopped for the night at the first point she found that someone had left her a can of Vienna Sausage. She understood and as she crawled out of the derelict car the next morning she tucked a candy bar in the glove compartment. Most nights were spent in abandoned cars that were off the highway.

The closer she walked to the pickup location, the more she understood that whoever was going to meet her there must test her to see that she was a true believer who had not taken the mark before they would show her the rest of the way to the hiding place. There was a measure of comfort in that knowledge. That would mean that she would be among true brethren.

She remembered in the instructions the old water tower with the strange spray painted graffiti. It was easy enough to see, a blue eye looking through an knothole in a fence. Someone was really talented and also dedicated to hang upside down from the scaffold to paint that eye. It blended really well with the rest of the graffiti but also stood out. Her mind wandered as she wondered who the artist was, and how he could possibly have not fallen. She had followed the instructions well, and had stayed just off the main roads and walked through vacant lots and woods keeping hidden as best as she could all the while paralleling the main road from her home in Marietta. She knew that the water tower was in Dawsonville and the hideout was several miles further. She just did not know which direction and how much further. That would be up to the people who would meet her.

Her family had passed through Dawsonville many times before, but never on foot. She began to realize all the things that she had missed in her life while driving by at 55 miles per hour. Those days were over now, and walking was the normal mode of transportation for almost everyone.

Rick had told her to wear tan and brown clothing to blend in with the fall colors. She had no camo clothing, but Rick had advised against that too, "If you wear camo people will suspect you ARE trying to hide". She was glad that it was fall so that her trek would not have to be in the heat of summer. Summers in northern Georgia could be sweltering and her water supply would have been long gone by now had it been July or August. Rick had promised that there would be plenty of drinkable water at the bugout location. She could only hope that she would actually know someone there, but the Holy Spirit kept reminding her that the people there would all be members of the Body of Christ. They would be her brothers and sisters. Surely she would be able to make friends easily. Only a day ago she had a scare while walking on the outskirts of a little one-stoplight town that caused her to think that she might not make it to the meeting zone. An unmarked white cargo van had slowed and almost stopped as she crouched in the bushes. She cowered in fear as she thought about them asking to scan her arm and then taking her in when they found out she did not have the invisible tattoo. Since the New Depression the police and other authorities had to revert to whatever transportation they could utilize. You could not tell what they would be riding in, so it was best to not trust any vehicle on the roadways. Besides truckers and public transportation, they were the only ones who had access to fuel anyway. Untold thousands of vehicles now sat unused in garages and driveways. In the earlier stages of the New Depression car theft was rampant, but now with no fuel available there was no longer a market for stolen cars. This was a whole new world with constantly changing ways. The basics of life such as food and water were more sought after than anything else. Shelter was for the most part available to anyone. Simply find an abandoned home. The foreclosure rate had been so high that it literally was the final nail in the coffin for the old banking system. Even people who had been able to stay in their own homes were now basically squatters.

The President had tried to turn all the foreclosed properties into rentals, but the economy was so bottomed out that people could not even afford cheap rent. Many municipal water systems were now defunct as entire cities were bankrupt. The fortunate few who were still employed found their incomes far from sufficient and almost the entire population depended on the shambles of a government for necessities which hardly ever came.

The van had slowed down and then she actually heard the men mutter something and then they drove on. She stayed behind the bush for a few more moments before moving on, but now her trek moved even deeper in the woods. She had to be more careful, and added that thought to her constant prayers. The important thing was to keep the highway in sight. That was her source of direction, and she must maintain a line of sight to hold her on course. Rick had instructed her to walk about a mile north of the water tower and look for an abandoned farmhouse with a old windmill by it. Knowing that she might get confused about North/South he had told her specific landmarks along the line of sight. Her pace was more hurried now and she quickly scurried along lining up the details from memory and soon she was at the pickup location.

In her sight now, the run down house was a welcome sight. Sharon wondered how many years had passed since a coat of paint had been applied. The old metal roof that once shone silver was now a shade of rust similar to a coffee stain. Half of the huge wraparound porch had caved in and the rest was questionable to walk on. But however bad the condition of the old structure there was a certain allure knowing that she would be close to ending this trek. Her backpack had been reduced to one granola bar and a half bottle of water. There had not been any creeks or water sources to use her filter bottle for the past day. She was thirsty right now, but taking no chances on her only known source of water.

Walking through the sparse underbrush caused her to think back a decade ago when as a girl of twelve she would play in a similar place behind her family home. Tears coursed down her cheeks as she thought about the rest of her family who had taken the invisible tattoo. The words of her father still rang in her ears. "You need to put this foolishness aside and get the tattoo with the rest of us. If you don't, then I'm afraid you wont be able to stay here. You will be causing trouble for the rest of us." Those words were a shock to her knowing that only a few months prior her father was a deacon in their home church. Now he had walked away from everything that he had instilled in his family. His faith was shipwreck, having believed that somehow Jesus would 'rapture' out believers before anything really bad happened. She didn't know which was harder, leaving hearth and home, or watching as her parents gave up hope.

Scriptures flooded her mind constantly now as she realized that Jesus had foretold all of this in detail, but so many she knew had followed after teachers who corrupted the truth. She remembered that Jesus said that your own family would turn against you. Brother against brother and father against son. All of Matthew chapter 24 was constantly being played out before her. The worst part of this whole living nightmare was that her family had now taken the mark and their names had been blotted out of the Book of Life. There was no getting around that scripture. It was clear cut and spoke volumes in one sentence.

As she brushed aside yet another tear, and a low hanging limb, she began to pray once again and thank God for sending Rich her way. He had been the youth leader for a while at Harmony Worship Center, but had been asked to step down from leadership because he began to teach that the antichrist must be revealed before the rapture could take place. Nearly the entire church simply refused to hear his teaching. They believed the pastor who taught that

nothing else had to be fulfilled prophetically before Jesus would rapture the church. That went hand in hand with the teaching that God would somehow not allow believers to suffer persecution. Rick had been allowed to stay in the church and did so simply because of his love for all the young people. He simply could no longer have a voice.
A local coffee shop became a new base for teaching and he had soon developed a small group that came to believe the clear teaching that came from the Bible about the end times. Sharon was a part of that small group. She still lived at home but her parents gave her freedoms since she was now an adult. It was accepted that she could choose where she went as long as she remained a member at Harmony. After all, Rick was a dedicated believer and what could be the harm. Little did they know that their daughter would be the only one in their family who knew the truth of the end times.
Sharon wondered why Rick was not coming with her as she was preparing to leave. His only reply was "a 'watchman' could not leave his post until the King relieved him of it." So far he had not heard that message from the Lord. Rick would be staying behind in hiding,

but all the time in plain sight seeing if he could find others who had not taken the mark. He was sure that there would be more. Sharon muttered a special prayer for him as she came to the edge of the woods by the farmhouse. She was sure this was the right farmhouse, for just as Rick had mentioned there was a barn that looked much newer than the house. And of course there was the windmill. How many places would actually have a windmill?

Quite some time passed before she left the solace of the woods to venture forth towards the barn. She had scanned every square inch of the property several times looking for any movement. She had to be sure that all looked safe before she would take those steps into the open. The bush-hiding incident from a day ago was fresh in her mind. The sun had about two hours before setting when she finally felt safe and stepped out. She made her way to the barn quickly, stopping at every bush or anything she could hide behind. Soon she was at the western wall of the barn, crouching down and pausing before walking around towards the big opening where double doors had once hung. Along the side she passed a window and chanced a look in but the darkness of the barn allowed no glimpse of anything of the interior. As she scurried around the corner she saw the big door opening and slowed, leery of walking in too quickly. Standing by the door for what seemed an eternity she finally looked in only to be grabbed by the collar of her shirt and pulled inside. Another hand covered her mouth to prevent the scream that had formed in her throat and she soon found herself against the wall with more than one set of hands holding her there.

The thoughts that flashed through her mind in a millisecond overwhelmed her. Caught, betrayed and soon to be taken in and ordered to take the mark or pay the consequences. Deny her faith and bow to the new One World religion or be sent who knows where or even suffer death. As her mind reeled, her body reached its limit and she slumped in total faint only to be caught by the same hands that had pinned her.

* * * * *

The splash of water on her face roused her quickly, only to find that her hands were bound and a gag was over her mouth. She could tell that it was still daylight but could not make out the faces of several people hovered over her. As she struggled against the bonds a voice spoke softly but urgently. "Please don't scream and we will take the gag from you. We don't want anyone to know we are here. We need to ask you some questions and I promise we wont hurt you. OK?"

Sharon nodded her head and felt small hands reach behind her head to untie the knot. "Those are the hands of a child", she thought. Her eyes were beginning to take in more of her surroundings now and she could tell that there was a man, woman and what looked like a girl around ten years old.

"Why are you here?" the man asked.

Sharon began to speak but stopped quickly. She wasn't even sure who these people were and sure wasn't about to tell them the real reason without knowing something about them. "I was about to ask you the same thing".

The man spoke again, "We need to know if you are by yourself and why...." but was interrupted by the woman.

"Be easy on her, can't you see she is scared". "Listen, we know why we are here and I'm thinking that you are here for the same reason. Let me ask you this, are you a believer?"

"Yes." There was no harm in answering that.

"I mean a believer that really believes in Jesus." the woman asked.

"Yes, I am a believer. A real one." Sharon knew that nothing would be revealed by that admission. There were plenty of people who had taken the mark who insisted that they were still believers, that nothing had changed.

The woman looked to the man and said, "Aaron, why else would she be here if not for the same reason as us?"

Once again the man who had just been named spoke, "You know my name now" as he glanced at the woman "and her name is Carry. This is our daughter Chelsea and we are here waiting to meet someone who will take us to the next place on our journey."

Sharon asked "You mean the bugout place?"

"Yes, that is what they call it. I'm sure it is not far from here, maybe somewhere in the hills over there. How far did you travel?"

"This is my fifth day of walking. I think it is close to sixty miles from my home. And I am tired. Could you untie my hands please?"

As Chelsea and Carry loosed her from her bonds Aaron began to ask about who had sent her. The sun was beginning to set over the hills to their west now and darkness was slowly taking hold. He told her that his family had spent last night in the barn, waiting for someone to come. He knew that whoever came would do so at night so that chances of being spotted were diminished. That is why they had surprised Sharon, as they thought with her coming in the day that she might have been working with the authorities.

No fire was lit that night or any other night, for obvious reasons. A good blanket was a necessity and Sharon had hers rolled up and hung below her backpack. Rick had cautioned her well about a fire and many other things that would draw attention. Of course there were so many transient people anyway that she could have blended in, but the risks of associating with people you did not know where manifold. It was very easy for a few people to overpower one and then simply divide the spoils.

It was not possible to spot someone who had not taken the mark. The tattoo was invisible and organic. It was a hybrid technology that actually infused with the person's DNA. Only a special scanner could read the mark and those units were all held by authorities and merchants. Once the mark was taken a week or so would pass before the body would actually imprint the genetic information within the tattoo. Thousands had refused the mark, not always because of religious conviction or biblical insight but some simply because they felt it was the last invasion of what little freedom was left to them. Many had said that they would rather die and if the stories were true, that very thing was taking place on a great scale.

Those who refused and were not true believers had turned to thievery and remained hidden. If they could not buy their only recourse was to starve or steal. The prison system was a shambles and life inside them was a pure nightmare. Most people were killed shortly after being interned, unless they were stronger and more streetwise than the criminals inside. And the threadbare force that guarded the prisoners were not much better, to the point of turning their heads and not saying anything. Control was a long gone matter other than just opening fire into the yard. Stories had emerged of guards killing scores at one time. Mass graves were to be found behind most prisons.

Aaron suggested they huddle together for warmth. Sharon combined her blanket with theirs as Chelsea snuggled between her and Carry. Aaron was going to stay up til midnight and then wake Carry to watch. Both had agreed that Sharon needed a full night's rest. That was something that had eluded her for the past week.

Shortly after dark Aaron came and woke everyone. "Someone is coming, be quiet and get behind the door and be ready to run." Sharon was quick to her feet and made her way to the window on the north side where Aaron had gone after waking them. The moon was half full and hidden behind the sparse clouds, but still you could see two figures making their way to the barn. She and Aaron quickly moved to their position behind the door after grabbing blankets and packs. The four weary fugitives waited in anticipation as they could hear footsteps that were now in a trot coming up to the door. Just outside the door they stopped and the half moon came out from behind the cloud revealing a slight shadow of the two figures.

A voice called out barely above a whisper, "If someone is in there don't worry, we are friends." Sharon wanted to say something but was not able to speak. Aaron stood with his arms wide in front of the three as if he was shielding them. The voice called again, "We aren't coming in, but if you can hear us we will wait for you to come out." Aaron stood still and Sharon could see him shaking his head as if to tell them to be quiet. He turned and looked at them and motioned for them not to move, then crept towards the door. He stopped short from going out.

Sharon heard one of the figures outside mumble something and then she heard the footsteps begin to walk away. She was amazed that she could hear their steps because her heart was beating so loudly that it was drumming inside her ears. As they walked away Aaron moved so that he could peek out of the doorway. He let them walk away across toward the house and then walked up behind them. His first thoughts were that if he were wrong about them, then at least he would be far enough away from the barn that the women would be able to make a break and run.

"Here I am" he called to the figures, who stopped where they were. They slowly turned to face him. Sharon was not able to not know what was going on and had moved to look out the door. She saw them talk for a few minutes and then embrace each other with back slapping hugs. Her heart slowed finally as she knew that she would be alright. The three women stood in the door as Aaron and the two men walked back.

"We must hurry. Make sure nothing is left behind. The barn must look untouched. Grab your belongings and follow us" the taller of the two said. Quickly they followed orders and soon were walking swiftly north towards the hills.

* * * * *

When the group arrived at the final location it was well after midnight. Sharon had been slapped in the face by branches and stumbled twice in the dark, but at last the journey was over. Dalonegha had been the site of the very first gold rush in North America. Many mine shafts had been dug before the gold played out and became a tourist attraction of sorts some years before, but since the New Depression no one had money for such entertainment. Theme parks that once had hosted thousands on a summer day now stood derelict. The mine shafts that were never open to the public and tended to be more remote were now a gathering place for believers waiting on the rapture and avoiding the mark.

Sharon had found her new temporary earthly home. Blending in was not a huge problem for Sharon. Being the oldest child had made her take on more of a servant role as she helped her mother raise her little sister. She simply dove in to whatever task needed another set of hands. As the days passed she noticed how the believers at the bugout worked as a team without anyone having to be in total charge. For the first time in her life she felt as if she were part of a church body that was truly organic, that really cared for each other in every aspect. Everyone did what they were good at and she soon found that she was very good at washing clothes in the nearby creek. She actually enjoyed the labor of serving others in this fashion. Washing clothes gave her time to talk with the other women as she worked.

Every evening the gatherers would leave out under the cover of darkness. Theirs was a risky job, spreading out into the nearby community foraging for foodstuffs and basic items for life to carry on. The remote location that they were in meant that the trip actually would last three days. They would travel only at night and "cold camp" during the days. Most of the communities were a nights trek and then some. What they gathered was scant as they were mostly raiding garbage piles. Thievery was not a choice among the believers. God always led the gatherers to the best locations and there always seemed to be something that had been disposed of that was still of use. The hunters were adept at their craft, using bow and arrow, snares and traps to catch all manner of game. Anything that moved was eaten by the hungry believers at the hideout. Small animals would be placed in a large pot and used to make stew or soup. Sharon even enjoyed a daily cup of pine needle tea. There was plenty of fresh water that ran from springs in the rocky hillside. Life was hard, but good at the camp.

Each evening as dusk rolled in the group would gather towards the end of the mine shaft for a meeting. Sharon enjoyed these meetings that always included a prayer time and singing. No sermons were needed, as they were living sermons each day. Rather, anyone who wanted to encourage the flock would speak in turns, sharing whatever God had laid on their spirits. It was during the evening meeting several weeks after Sharon arrived that someone new brought the news that Rick had been captured. He had just given them directions to the barn when the police walked around the corner and asked to scan them. Rick had told them to run and then turned and ran at the officers and tackled both of them at once. The two teens ran off a short distance and then watched as Rick was handcuffed and escorted towards the police station. Sharon wept that night as a special prayer was offered for Rick. She thought she knew the two teens and made her way to them as the dark took over the night. They all had something in common beyond being believers. They owed a debt to Rick, the watchman that God had sent their way. They hugged for a long time and all wept together until the tears slowed. Sharon led them back to her little corner of the mine close to Aaron's family. The three young ladies all huddled under their collective blankets and slept soundly.

Ellie and Barbara stuck to Sharon like glue. They were all from Marietta and even had some of the same teachers in school. The two girls looked up to her in many ways because she was slightly older and had endured leaving her family just as they had. Soon they knew almost everything about each other. Ellie was the first to notice Sharon's special hand. Sharon had been born with only three fingers on her left hand. She always joked that she could never marry because she didn't have a ring finger. Ellie asked "Does it bother you?" only to stop, realizing that Sharon might not want to talk about it.

"No, not at all. It's hard to miss something you never had. Most people don't notice until I point it out."

"Do you ever wish you had it?" Ellie asked. "I'm sorry, am I bothering you?"

Sharon laughed and then tears began to form as she said " If I could have it, I would trade it for my family to be here right now." That night bonded the three of them together forever. All had left family behind. All knew the consequences that their parents must face for taking the mark.

* * * * *

The wars had come shortly after the peace pact had been signed by Israel and her surrounding neighbors. It seemed like war just broke out all over the globe after that day. It was as if peace had been stolen from mankind. Only in Israel was there peace. Everywhere there was fighting as the 1st Seal had been opened in Heaven.
People were killing each other over basic necessities. People were killing each other over a place to live. People were killing each other over nothing sometimes. People had simply gone crazy. If you had food, people would kill you for it. Wars unlike had been known before began to plague the earth. The 2nd Seal had been opened in heaven.
 Then the fragile economies of the world crashed even further into depression than they had ever before and rich and poor alike struggled to even buy food. There was not food to go around any longer. People were dying of starvation in record numbers. Fuel was a precious

commodity and farmer's tractors sat idle. Infrastructures of governments had failed and people were left to defend themselves and to find a way of provision as best as they could. The 3nd Seal had been opened in heaven.

After a few months an unthinkable fact become known. Over a fourth of the world's population was gone! Almost two billion souls no longer walked the earth. The 4th Seal had been opened in Heaven.

 The earthquakes and natural disasters had become more severe than ever since the signing of the peace pact. However, it seemed like around Israel there was a hedge. The peace had taken and was working. For the first time in centuries Israel and her Arab neighbors were not fighting. Jonah Buvaldi had seemingly risen from nowhere and had become a world leader. When he spoke, people listened and most found that they could not argue with his intellect. His plan was working. And now he was saying that he had a similar plan for the entire world that would stop all the wars and finally bring peace. The estimates of how many people had been killed during the recent wars was staggering. People were listening to him. Governments were slowly turning around to see that there was a chance that he was right. After all, he had caused peace to reign in the Middle East.

He had been the greatest promoter of tolerance that the world had ever seen. Major religions were coming together, prepared in advance by compromising teachers who proclaimed that all paths lead towards God. Most of these teachers were flamboyant and spoke with swelling words that the people wanted to hear. For a long time now the church had been taught a doctrine that causes believers to want God because of what He can do for them, rather than what can they do for Him. The Church of Jesus Christ had been primed for a one world religion and didn't even see it coming. Pastors that preached the truth found themselves without a flock. Some bowed to the pressure and went along with the teaching of the 'giants of the faith'.

Now the great religion had a life of it's own, swallowing up everything in it's path. Soon the religious leaders began to promote Jonah's plan for peace. After all, it was built on tolerance. Political leaders of bankrupt nations were desperate for anything that would protect their livelihoods and keep them in office. One by one they agreed to the plan and within a year the whole known world was under a single monetary system and marking everyone to give them the privilege to buy or sell. Then, the persecution began. The plan for peace and restoration set in stone by the leaders of the nations included the marking system to qualify people to buy and sell. Anyone not taking the mark were imprisoned and eventually murdered. The 5th Seal had been opened in Heaven.

* * * * *

The day of the great earthquake was an event like none other. The center of the earthquake was off Indonesia on the Pacific floor. The ripples were felt all over the world and the tsunami that radiated out from it reached as far as the Americas with one hundred seventy five foot waves. Entire cities were swept out to sea all around the Pacific basin. Major volcanoes began erupting and spewing ash by the ton into the atmosphere. Fires were burning uncontrollably where the hot ash had ignited forests. Sharon was washing clothes with the other women when the creek actually stopped running for a few moments.

Birds stopped singing and it seemed as if the whole world stopped.

Sharon never went anywhere without her backpack, and after the shaking stopped she reached in and pulled out her bible. Turning to Revelation she read a passage that Rick had shared with her.

Rev 6:12-17 And I beheld when he had opened the sixth seal, and, lo, there was a great earthquake; and the sun became black as sackcloth of hair, and the moon became as blood;   And the stars of heaven fell unto the earth, even as a fig tree casteth her untimely figs, when she is shaken of a mighty wind.   And the heaven departed as a scroll when it is rolled together; and every mountain and island were moved out of their places.   And the kings of the earth, and the great men, and the rich men, and the chief captains, and the mighty men, and every bondman, and every free man, hid themselves in the dens and in the rocks of the mountains;   And said to the mountains and rocks, Fall on us, and hide us from the face of him that sitteth on the throne, and from the wrath of the Lamb: For the great day of his wrath is come; and who shall be able to stand?

She remembered the watchman's teaching that when the great earthquake shook and the sky became like the scriptures spoke of that the rapture was soon. Jesus would be coming and every eye would see Him! She knew that everything that occurred so far was not God's wrath. She knew that was to happen later, after the rapture. She wept and rejoiced and the women with her joined in worship.

* * * * *

In the days that followed the great earthquake there was a strange phenomenon that took place. The winds ceased. All over the world there was a stillness of the air. Four great angels had been given charge of the winds and told not to allow the wind to blow. The whole world grew stagnant and the ash from the great volcanoes settled. Night had almost come in the mountains of north Georgia when the next event happened. All over the world darkness began to take hold. It was not from the ash but from something else that had happened once before. When Jesus hung suspended on the torture tree we call the cross darkness had permeated the earth. It was no eclipse nor was there a natural reason. It was a spiritual darkness that had crossed into the natural realm. Now it was happening again. Angels began to slowly appear in the skies of the whole earth. It was like they were fading in from nothingness. And as they began to appear there were so many of them that they blocked out the sun, turning it black like an eclipse that was everywhere at the same time. On the other side of the world the moon was turning a reddish hue as it was being blocked also. The stars were no longer seen. Angels were everywhere in the skies and people stood in shock with their mouths hanging open. Others fell to the ground from heart failure at the sight. Lightning began to flash beginning in the east and reaching with long fingers to the west circling the globe. Then a blast from a horn literally shook the earth. No one could tell where the sound came from. Everyone on the earth heard it with equal volume. The earth stood silent for a few moments. Then the screams started again as the angels began to move towards the earth. Some people were running to hide and others stood transfixed by fear. The angels began plummeting to the ground and sea and standing momentarily as people were rising up from graves and oceans. Other angels swept down among the living and and began to take people. They would simply touch the person and swiftly both the angel and the person would fly upwards.   In a single moment if was over. Most people never had a chance to move, but the sight of what happened would never leave them. The most sobering part was when the angels moved so quickly out of the sky, all could see that there was a lone figure in the clouds. It was the Son of Man, Christ coming back for his elect!

Sharon was standing at the entrance to the mine with the others. There were close to four hundred at the bugout. Almost everyone there began to lift their hands as the angels descended and touched them. Sharon felt a flash of energy go through her and as she was being led skyward by her angel she realized that her body had changed. She felt new. Yes, that was the only word she could come up with. New. And now a stranger feeling came over her as she realized that her thoughts had no fear in them. All fear was gone and there was peace like she had never known. She closed her eyes and realized something else. She knew. She simply knew things that she had not understood in the bible before. It was all becoming plain to her in an instant.

Everything happened so fast as they rose skyward that she almost didn't notice a truly miraculous event had happened. She had all of her fingers on her hand! Her new body was complete and whole in every way! And there in the clouds above the earth she saw Him, her Beloved, her Healer. He was waiting for His Bride and His Bride was flying to him carried on angel's wings.

* * * * *

Section I

In The Thick Of It

The early church was married to poverty, prisons and persecutions. Today, the church is married to prosperity, personality, and popularity.

Leonard Ravenhill

Centuries ago, when Thomas a' Kempis was shown the wealth of the Church, he was told, "No longer can the Church say, 'Silver and gold, have I none.'"
To which a' Kempis replied, "Neither can she say, "Arise, take up thy bed and walk!"

Please understand that this book is not a diatribe against the modern, western church. However, this book cannot relay the message that 'must needs' go forth without touching the subject of the condition to which the church has degraded. If you are a member of a missional church that is on fire and serving God understand that I am in no way singling out any one local church or denomination but rather speaking of the western church as a whole. The enemy of our souls has done his work well and the church is in a quandary. He has cleverly led many astray into various teachings that are not of God. We have strayed down too far many wrong paths. Below I list some observations that clearly outline one thing: It is ALL ABOUT JESUS CHRIST, and nothing else.

- Rather than a 'purpose driven life' we needed a 'Person driven life'. The Person is Christ. We don't need a purpose other than His purpose, which was to come and die. He calls us to die as well. Die to self, the world and all that the world offers.
- Rather than having a 'worship experience' to carry you through the week, live the week as a worship experience.
- You cannot go to church if you are the church. Our vocabulary reflects the degree of our commitment. Examine your vocabulary, test yourself. Count how many times in a week that you use the word church as a geographic location instead of its true meaning.

> Rather than attempting to get people to 'come to church', be the church to them. Take the church with you at all times.

Depending on the time in which you are reading this book the true church of Jesus Christ may be underground, suffering persecution by the system controlled by the beast.(More on him later) If that is so, I can guarantee you that the church is more alive than it has been in years. (Consider the underground church in China) If you are reading this book before the 70th week of Daniel (1) and the Beginnings of Sorrows (2) then you have a wonderful opportunity to tell others to help them to prepare for the coming persecution.

You may find yourself totally 'in the thick' of events that you do not understand. This book was written to help you deal with and comprehend the events happening so fast that you cannot keep up with them. Some of these events no man will understand in this life, but will only be able to grasp them after the resurrection. (3)

The first section of this book will assist you in understanding how you may not have known the truth of

End Time events. The second section will begin with what you should know in order to keep up with the passing and future events as they transpire.

1. Daniel 9:24-27
2. Matthew 24:8
3. 1 Corinthians 15:51

How Could This Happen?

If you are reading this book and you find yourself smack in the middle of all hell breaking loose, allow me to assure you that it is, indeed, *"all hell"* breaking loose. Satan (Lucifer, the dragon) is furious because he knows that his time is short, and he is taking it out on anyone who truly loves Jesus!

"Therefore rejoice, ye heavens, and ye that dwell in them. Woe to the inhabiters of the earth and of the sea! for the devil is come down unto you, having great wrath, because he knoweth that he hath but a short time." (Revelation 12:12)

All around you there is war, famine and economic collapse of a magnitude that you never conceived could happen. You are terribly confused because your favorite prophecy teacher assured you "nothing else had to be fulfilled" before Jesus came and raptured the church. You are thinking, "surely God would not pour out His wrath on believers" and in that thought you are correct. If you are a believer, faithfully loving and serving Christ then you are not experiencing God's wrath. God's wrath is reserved for the wicked. Carefully reread the verse above to see that you are feeling the **wrath of Satan**. God has not given up on you. God will not pour out His wrath on his children.

Now a new menace is raising it's ugly head, and by the time you read this book it may very well have begun. I am speaking about the persecution of followers of Christ in nations that were previously very tolerant of Christians. It is really a miracle at all that you are reading this book. I'm speaking prophetically now saying that there may be censorship as you have never known before. You may have been handed this book by a trusted brother or sister in the Lord. But the real deal is that while you read this book, you may be doing so in a manner that no one knows what you are doing.

The Beast system is in place. All religions have basically morphed into one. For years this religious system has been gradually set in motion by the enemy as pastors and teachers either watered down the Truth, or preached heresy while countless minions followed. Most of these teachers and many of their followers have either taken the mark or will take the mark. (Depends on when you read this) In the late nineties many prominent pastors and teachers began to teach that we should work together with other faiths and join in programs with them for the benefit of humankind. The teaching quickly became popular because it was cleverly tied to the prosperity message as well as the 'tolerance' message that invaded the church.

Following another heresy is easy when you are already following one.

In the following paragraphs I will give you the layman's synopsis of what may ***not*** have been taught to you. This may be the first time you are hearing this. Or it may be that you have heard it but rejected the truth because you desired to be raptured out before any calamity came your way. What I am speaking of is the 6th Seal rapture teaching. I first learned this important lesson during my own study of the Bible in 1976.

If you have a bible with you, I invite you to turn to The Revelation of Jesus Christ, chapter 6. This chapter begins with the opening of the first Seal. There are 7 Seals in all, and they coincide with the 7oth week of Daniel's Vision. When a 7 year peace accord is signed between Israel and her neighbors the 1st seal will be opened.

Seal 1 – Nations are conquered and brought in line by the one who sits on the White Horse. He is given the power to conquer.

Seal 2 – People begin to kill each other through wars, murders and mayhem as peace is removed from the earth. However, Israel will sit in peace with her Muslim neighbors as the rest of the world goes crazy.

Seal 3 – The economy tanks as it never has before, worldwide.

Seal 4 – Famine and pestilence accompanied by Death. One fourth of the world population is now dead or dying.

Seal 5 – Persecution of believers like never before. The system of the Beast becomes fully implemented as he takes control and sets out to destroy once and for all those who follow Christ.

Seal 6 – The greatest earthquake ever recorded. Let me emphasize the word EVER. The sun darkens as well as the stars, the moon turns to blood and the earth mourns because they know that the day of His wrath has come.

Chapter 6 concludes with verse 17 showing that now the wrath of the Lamb (God) is coming.

Revelation 6:15-17 And the kings of the earth, and the great men, and the rich men, and the chief captains, and the mighty men, and every bondman, and every free man, hid themselves in the dens and in the rocks of the mountains; (16) And said to the mountains and rocks, Fall on us, and hide us from the face of him that sitteth on the throne, and from the <u>wrath of the Lamb</u>: (17) For the great day of <u>his wrath is come</u>; and who shall be able to stand?

It is at this point that the rapture takes place as noted by the sudden appearance of great multitude of believers dressed in white, at the throne of God in chapter 7.

Revelation 7:9-17 After this I beheld, and, lo, a great multitude, which no man could number, of all nations, and kindreds, and people, and tongues, stood before the throne, and before the Lamb, clothed with white robes, and palms in their hands; (10) And cried with a loud voice, saying, Salvation to our God which sitteth upon the throne, and unto the Lamb. (11) And all the angels stood round about the throne, and about the elders and the four beasts, and fell before the throne on their faces, and worshipped God, (12) Saying, Amen: Blessing, and glory, and wisdom, and thanksgiving, and honour, and power, and might, be unto our God for ever and ever. Amen. (13) And one of the elders answered, saying unto me, **What are these which are arrayed in white robes?** and whence came they? (14) And I said unto him, Sir, thou knowest. And he said to me, These are they which **came out of great tribulation**, and have washed their robes, and made them white in the blood of the Lamb. (15) Therefore are they before the throne of God, and serve him day and night in his temple: and he that sitteth on the throne shall dwell among them. (16) They shall hunger no more, neither thirst any more; neither shall the sun light on them, nor any heat. (17) For the Lamb which is in the midst of the throne shall feed them, and shall lead them unto living fountains of waters: and God shall wipe away all tears from their eyes.

Understand that this is the first appearance of believers in the Revelation after chapter three ends with the letters to the churches. In chapter 7 a separate event occurs wherein 144,000 Jews are 'sealed' for protection against the wrath of God on earth. All other people who do not go in the rapture will have to face the wrath of God. What happens next is opening of the final Seal.

Seal 7 – Silence in Heaven for a half hour. Why silence? Because what is about to happen is so terrible that there must be a pause beforehand. Think of it as if you were about to take your first dive off the high dive, and paused at the edge before jumping to contemplate what was coming next.

Now comes the Wrath of God. My point to you is note all that has happened up to this point. All that has taken place is not God's Wrath, but is The Beginning Of Sorrows, and Satan's Wrath.

Revelation 12:12 Therefore rejoice, *ye* heavens, and ye that dwell in them. Woe to the inhabiters of the earth and of the sea! for the devil is come down unto you, <u>having great wrath</u>, because he knoweth that he hath but a short time.

Note above that Satan knows he only has a short time to do his damage. As I said before he has been busy setting up his system, and he has been using deceived ministers and teachers of God to 'aid and abet' the process!

As I was writing Walking Backwards a serious event happened within the church. I believe that it was not a coincidence but rather that God had it all timed to cement in my mind how important the message of the 6th Seal rapture is. God knows how to drive home a point with the perfect visual and auditory accompaniment. I also want you to know that God is with you through all this and He will give you the peace that passes all understanding as you Walk Backwards and possibly (highly likely) face persecution.

I listened as a popular radio teacher (James McDonald) backtracked and changed positions on a point of faith. He had heard from God and knew now that the 6th Seal rapture was the only accurate theology to teach. He began his show on a Monday with the preface that he knew that he was about to lose listeners, but had to tell the truth of what he had discovered. My spirit soared within me as I listened to his message. It was fantastic to witness a brother come to terms with being on the wrong path on a point of faith and then see him finding his way back. He took a full week of programming to ensure that the truth was told.

The following Saturday I was listening to another teacher (Jimmy DeYoung) on a different broadcast. He had a guest pastor on the show and they were speaking about how James McDonald was now teaching heresy. They called him by name on the air, and spoke about how he was bringing a spirit of fear into the church. The tirade went on for several minutes. I was torn between emotions. Part of me wanted to weep because of the men dragging this brother through the mud. But then another emotion arose as I listened with the spirit and heard the Word speaking in my heart.

Luke 6:22-23 Blessed are you when men shall hate you, and when they shall cut you off, and when they shall reproach you and shall cast out your name as evil, for the sake of the Son of Man. (23) Rejoice in that day and leap for joy. For behold, your reward is great in

Heaven. For so their fathers did according to these things to the prophets.

A man had decided to walk backwards when he discovered the truth that he was going down the wrong trail. I rejoiced with him. He rejected pride and humbled himself before his listeners, but more importantly, before God. My sadness turned to joy. It was painfully apparent to see who was the true brother and who was in the wrong.

This teacher knew that there were many walking with him. He knew that when he turned back and headed towards truth that some would not follow. He knew that some would walk with him but that others would not.

He found out quickly and exactly what people thought, thanks to his name being drug through the mud on a nationally syndicated broadcast. When you and I turn back to the truth, we can be assured that some who do not understand will inflict hurt. I say this to you not to discourage you, but to encourage you. Being armed with the truth is the most important part of preparation.

The rapture of the church will occur after the 6th Seal of Revelation is opened. Not before. This is plainly echoed by Jesus himself in Matthew 24. I want to take you there and show you the parallels between the Seals of Revelation and Matthew 24. What I highly suggest is that you the reader open your Bible to Revelation 6. Then as you read Matthew 24 below, I have noted in bold text where you should read in Revelation.

Mat 24:3-31 And as he sat upon the mount of Olives, the disciples came unto him privately, saying, Tell us, when shall these things be? and what *shall be* the sign of thy coming, and of the end of the world? (4) And Jesus answered and said unto them, Take heed that no man deceive you. (5) For many shall come in my name, saying, I am Christ; and shall deceive many. (6) And ye shall hear of wars and rumours of wars: see that ye be not troubled: for all these things must come to pass, but the end is not yet. (7) For nation shall rise against nation, and kingdom against kingdom: and there shall be famines, and pestilences, and earthquakes, in divers places. (8)

All these are the beginning of sorrows. **Seals 1 – 5, Verses 6 - 8**
(9) Then shall they deliver you up to be afflicted, and shall kill you: and ye shall be hated of all nations for my name's sake. (10) And then shall many be offended, and shall betray one another, and shall hate one another. (11) And many false prophets shall rise, and shall deceive many. (12) And because iniquity shall abound, the love of many shall wax cold. (13) But he that shall endure unto the end, the same shall be saved. **Seal 5, verses 9 - 13**

> (14) And this gospel of the kingdom shall be preached in all the world for a witness unto all nations; and then shall the end come. (15) When ye therefore shall see the abomination of desolation, spoken of by Daniel the prophet, stand in the holy place, (whoso readeth, let him understand:) (16) Then let them which be in Judea flee into the mountains: (17) Let him which is on the housetop not come down to take any thing out of his house: (18) Neither let him which is in the field return back to take his clothes. (19) And woe unto them that are

with child, and to them that give suck in those days! (20) But pray ye that your flight be not in the winter, neither on the sabbath day: (21) For then shall be great tribulation, such as was not since the beginning of the world to this time, no, nor ever shall be. (22) And except those days should be shortened, there should no flesh be saved: but for the elect's sake those days shall be shortened. (23) Then if any man shall say unto you, Lo, here *is* Christ, or there; believe *it* not. (24) For there shall arise false Christs, and false prophets, and shall shew great signs and wonders; insomuch that, if *it were* possible, they shall deceive the very elect. (25) Behold, I have told you before. (26) Wherefore if they shall say unto you, Behold, he is in the desert; go not forth: behold, *he is* in the secret chambers; believe *it* not. **Verses 14 – 26 are the persecution of the saints as a result of Seal 5** (27) For as the lightning cometh out of the east, and shineth even unto the west; so shall also the coming of the Son of man be. (28) For wheresoever the carcase is, there will the eagles be gathered together. (29) Immediately after the tribulation of those days shall the sun be darkened, and the moon shall not give her light, and the stars shall fall from heaven, and the powers of the heavens shall be shaken: (30) And then shall appear the sign of the Son of man in heaven: and then shall all the tribes of the earth mourn, and they shall see the Son of man coming in the clouds of heaven with power and great glory. (31) And he shall send his angels with a great sound of a trumpet, and they shall gather together his elect from the four winds, from one end of heaven to the other. **Verses 27 – 31, the 6th Seal culminating with the Rapture of the Church.**

It is understandable that you may have never heard of the 6th Seal rapture before now. The proper name for the study of End Time events is Eschatology. Most ministers shy from this study and subsequently do not teach on it for several reasons.

- ➤ They do not understand End Time events, so they do not teach them.

- They have a favorite eschatology teacher that is brought in from time to time to teach and lay the responsibility of teaching eschatology on him/her.
- They find that the timing of the rapture and other end time events can be controversial and do not wish to 'stir that pot', knowing that to do so may bring up questions that they cannot answer or possibly cause some in the flock to leave. In consequence they often make statements such as "Just be ready", and "It will all pan out".

To put it all in perspective the reasons that you have not heard the truth of the entire scripture concerning End Time events are manifold. First we must not point a finger, for when we do there are three more pointing back at us. The first part of the problem is US! As believers we are blessed to have the Holy Bible available to us and have the Spirit of God speak to us through the scriptures. But we find it so much easier to allow someone to figure it all out for us, do the research and the reading and then deliver it to us in a format that we like. (I call that being entertained with the Word) In the process of neglecting the precious Word of God we have allowed ourselves to be open to false teaching.

Most people read through The Revelation Of Jesus Christ and walk away shaking their head and saying that it is too confusing. What we so easily forget is that if we are born again, the very Author of the Word resides in us. But what we find so easy to do is heralded in this excerpt from Walking Backwards:

We as humans garner some measure of comfort in having someone to tell us what to do, rather than 'be responsible' for our own actions. This is why the ***faith*** called Christianity became the ***religion*** called Christianity. It didn't take long for this to transpire. All that was needed was for the apostles and those who had witnessed Christ to pass on and be removed from the scene. Soon the old order of works was in place again and faith was relegated to what the priest (minister) told you to do. Salvation depended on the word of the priest and no longer the Word of the Lord. Just a few generations passed and Christianity was the official religion of the state (Rome).

Down through time since then we have had reformations of one sort or another that included Martin Luther and various others who railed against the machine known as orthodoxy. But in the end many of the same principles that Paul and Peter warned us against remain in place even to this day.

It is the mindset of at least 90% of the church that we must have an educated minister in charge of the flock. This man must have a resume that indicates his level of study, work experience and last, but not least – the approval of men. In other words he is treated as a doctor, lawyer or other professional and is rated by the the fancy lettering and signatures on the document hanging on the wall in his office.

Understand that I am not railing against ministers. I possess a certificate of ordination from a well respected affiliation. However, that gives me no precedence over others who do not have a parchment hanging on the wall. It is the duty of all believers to be good disciples (students). It is our obligation to prepare not only for the present day but for the future. After all, part of "Watching and praying" is knowing what to watch for.

1Timothy 4:13 Till I come, give attendance to reading, to exhortation, to doctrine.

Revelation 1:3 Blessed *is* he that readeth, and they that hear the words of <u>this prophecy</u>, and keep those things which are written therein: for the time *is* at hand.

Jesus clearly wants us to be prepared. Return to Matthew 24 and see his warnings to believers.

Mat 24:4 And Jesus answered and said unto them, **Take heed** that no man deceive you.

Mat 24:25 Behold, I have **told you before**.

Mat 24:42 **Watch therefore**: for ye know not what hour your Lord doth come.

Mat 24:44 Therefore **be ye also ready**: for in such an hour as ye think not the Son of man cometh.

I think it should be clear now that we are to be students of prophecy. The 44th verse particularly haunts me in behalf of believers everywhere. You see, one of the greatest deceptions being taught by teachers today is to "Just be ready, because no man knows the day or the hour". This is tied to verse 42, but the sad part is that in verse 44 Jesus clarifies what he said in verse 42. Allow me to expound on that verse.

Be ready. Make yourself ready. He will not come as a thief in the night to those **who are** watching and ready. He will be that thief in the night to those who are **unprepared**. The hour in which He is coming will not be be the hour that YOU think, but it will be the hour that is appointed by the Father.

Understand a key point that you cannot deviate from and be safe. The rapture of the church will not occur until the Abomination of Desolation occurs!

2Thessolonians 2:1-4 Now we beseech you, brethren, by the coming of our Lord Jesus Christ, and *by* our **gathering together unto him**, (2) That ye be not soon shaken in mind, or be troubled, neither by spirit, nor by word, nor by letter as from us, as that the day of Christ is at hand. (3) Let no man deceive you by any means: for *that day shall not come*, except there come a falling away first, and that **man of sin be revealed,** the son of perdition; (4) Who opposeth and exalteth himself above all that is called God, or that is worshipped; so that he as God sitteth in the temple of God, shewing himself that he is God.

Paul also encourages us about watching and being prepared.

1Thessolonians 5:1-6 But of the times and the seasons, brethren, ye have no need that I write unto you. (2) For yourselves know perfectly that the day of the Lord so cometh as a thief in the night. (3) For when they shall say, Peace and safety; then sudden destruction cometh upon them, as travail upon a woman with child; and they shall not escape. (4) But ye, brethren, are not in darkness, that that day should overtake you as a thief. (5) Ye are all the children of light, and the children of the day: we are not of the night, nor of darkness. (6) Therefore let us not sleep, as *do* others; but let us watch and be sober.

So, in the end when you ask the question "How could this happen?" you must understand that the church was not prepared. In the next chapter we enter into some of the teachings that have caused the church to be in a state of unpreparedness.

1st Timothy DOD
Doctrines Of Demons

At the beginning of this chapter I must offer this statement. I am not here to tear down men. I am here to expose doctrines that are being/have been taught in the church that have steered people away from the truth. Demons have whispered these into the ears of teachers who have taken the seed and watered it until a harvest of heresy has been reaped. It is not the men I concern myself with as God will deal with all of us for our own sins. Rather I concern myself with the doctrines themselves.

Unconditional Eternal Security

The premise that once you ask Jesus into your heart you are forever secure no matter what. There is nothing that you can do that will remove your salvation. While the truth is that there is no one, no thing, no time or place that can take your salvation, you remain your worst enemy on this one. You are the one who can remove your salvation. This is a damnable doctrine that allows you to live a life devoid of God and be 'OK' as long as some time in the past you said a prayer, got dunked in the pool and joined the 'church'. When questioned about this in application to someone who was 'born again' yet went on to be the greatest heathen ever known, the proponents of this doctrine will simply cop out and say that person was never truly saved. The truth is that even proponents and teachers of this doctrine vary in their versions. Paul declared that no demon, no person, no physical object, no power or no ruler could separate us from the love of God. In that list was no mention of ourselves. Every teacher of UES that I have posed the following question to did not have an answer. The question is, "Does that mean that once you become saved, you no longer have a choice?". In other words, does God **force you** to stay saved? The only answer to that I have ever received is "They were never saved to start with".

Rest assured, you are in charge of your salvation. You have every right to lay it down and live a life without God. You are not a puppet controlled by a God who will force you into a life of worshiping Him.

Judging

This is a favorite defense for those who believe that God simply allows everyone 'good' to go to heaven.

For decades, the news media, television, movies, and universities, have bombarded Christians with this message: don't judge lest you be judged. Let us discern the demonic spirit using this ploy. The wicked will never love anyone judging their rebellion against God. The world will hate you if you teach what Jesus taught. This is why so many are not willing to take a stand for righteousness anymore. *

You can simply quote a scripture to most people and they will accuse you of judging them. Most can quote the verse and tell you that Jesus said "judge not, lest you be judged", but always take that one verse out of context. Then there are those who cannot quote the verse but claim to know the principle and simply say "You're judging me".

Truth: We are to judge in order to keep ourselves pure. We are to always tell the truth. We are always to point others to Christ. We are always to make disciples of all

nations. We are to tell the Good News that there is salvation in Christ. We ARE to judge **within the church.**
1Co 5:11-13 But now I have written unto you not to keep company, if any man that is called a brother be a fornicator, or covetous, or an idolater, or a railer, or a drunkard, or an extortioner; with such an one no not to eat. (12) For what have I to do to judge them also that are without? <u>do not ye judge them that are within?</u> (13) But them that are without God judgeth. Therefore put away from among yourselves that wicked person.

Finally, understand that people who are in sin will begin to hate you when they are exposed to the truth. Especially those who claim to be a part of the church that are caught in sin.
John 15:19 If ye were of the world, the world would love his own: but because ye are not of the world, but I have chosen you out of the world, therefore the world hateth you.
Do not worry when you tell someone the truth (IN LOVE PLEASE) and they reject you and accuse you of judging them. The truth is the truth.

All Religions Lead To God

For you, the believer in Christ there is only one God. He is not the God of the Hindus, Muslims, or any other religion. There is only one way to Jehovah God and that is through His Son Jesus.

Joel Osteen pastors the largest congregation in America. Larry King asked him if other religious faiths are wrong for not believing in Christ. Shamelessly, Joel declares they are not wrong. That only God can judge their hearts. He cites Hinduism as an example. He believes Hindus aren't wrong for not believing in Jesus because of their sincerity and love for God. What God is he talking about? Hindus will worship a cow as God before worshiping Jesus. A person's sincerity or love for a pagan religion will never make it true. Hinduism is an evil deception that has sent billions to Hades *

The Manifest Sons Of God

This is one of the trickiest of late. Followers of this doctrine believe that they are little gods. Teachers of this doctrine began as the 'Faith' movement and include such as Creflo Dollar, Kenneth Copeland, Benny Hinn and others.

Healing evangelist Benny Hinn boldly teaches Christians are everything Jesus was, is, and ever shall be. He blindly proclaims all born of the Spirit aren't human. Such heresy is turning many believers away from the truth. Kenneth Copeland challenges a captivated audience you don't have God in you; you are God. He says he received this revelation from the Holy Spirit. The above teachers have brainwashed thousands of pastors to teach this heresy called, the Manifest Sons of God. Let's review the foundational lies of this heretical doctrine.

One, they teach Jesus became unholy on the cross by accepting the nature of Satan. God is unchangeable (Mal 3:6). The Word is the same yesterday, today, and forever (1 John 5:7, Heb.13:8). It is blasphemous to teach the holy Son of God became unholy (Heb. 13:12; 10:10

Two, they teach the Son of God died spiritually on the cross. The forgiveness of sins through His blood is only through the offering of His body on the cross (Heb. 10:10). Jesus did not have to die spiritually to bring redemption for those believing in Him (Col. 1:14

Three, they teach Jesus had to suffer in hell. The suffering of the sinless Lamb of God was enough (1 Pet. 3:18). To teach Jesus had to suffer in hell to secure eternal redemption is sacrilegious (Heb. 9:11-12

Four, they teach Jesus had to be born again spiritually. The Christ triumphed over all principalities and powers by physically dying on the cross (Col. 2:14-15). Their declaration Jesus became a sinner and was reborn spiritually is a lie from Satan.

Five, they teach this was the only way Jesus could defeat the Devil. Teaching the Son of God could only defeat the Devil by being born again is a blatant assault on the divinity of Christ (Heb. 10:10). This is why their followers believe they can become divine Sons of God (John 10:33). No where in scripture is such blasphemy taught. *

I assure you that you are not a god in the same sense that Jehovah is God.

This next portion will inflame some and will free some (who have ears to hear). Lets go to scripture.

Orthodox Religions

These include all religions that place as much emphasis on traditions as scripture. Most orthodox religions claim to trace their development back to the apostles and Paul. Most are Catholic in nature or have their roots in Catholicism. Most share traditions that include the following things that Paul warned about.

1Timothy 4:1-3 Now the Spirit speaketh expressly, that in the latter times some shall depart from the faith, giving heed to seducing spirits, and <u>doctrines of devils</u>; (2) <u>Speaking lies in hypocrisy</u>; having their <u>conscience seared with a hot iron</u>; (3) <u>Forbidding to marry</u>, *and commanding* to abstain from meats, which God hath created to be received with thanksgiving of them which believe and know the truth.

In the verses above we see several points. The most dangerous part of this is in verse two where we see that the ones who speak the lies end up with their conscience seared. When something of an organic nature is seared, what is contained within is held captive. When you place a big juicy steak on the grill, you sear both sides so that the juices contained within don't run out. It is similar to the searing of the conscience in that what is contained within remains. The only way to release the juices/remove what is within is to use a sharp instrument to cut open the seared object.

With a steak, the normal apparatus is a steak knife. With a seared conscience only the Word of God (sharper than a two edged sword) will open the person to allow the lies out. Now let us tackle the two lies that are spoken of here.

> **Forbidding to Marry:** Where in the Word of God can you find evidence that (in this case) a priest is not to marry? I assure you, nowhere. This is a man-

made tradition that has caused untold grief within the Body of Christ. Forbidding men to marry opens the door for sin. Am I saying that all priests of orthodox religions fall to sin because they are not allowed to marry? No, that would be a baseless accusation. However, as we have evidenced in recent years with the rise of the media system of television and rapid, instantaneous communication, we have seen far too many cases of these very ones who were not allowed to marry diving off into crimes ranging from fornication to pedophilia. Chances are far greater that the people damaged by this tradition of men would be far less if these men were allowed to have wives. Also, the reverse of this is true with women who are forbidden to marry. Remember, nowhere in scripture can you find Christ forbidding ministers/priests to marry.

- **Commanding to Abstain From Meats**: Every Friday around the world people are told by canon to abstain from certain foods. Nowhere in scripture do we find that practice. It is only revealed in the canon and traditions of orthodoxy.

These are only two of the practices of orthodox church that have no scriptural basis whatsoever. To delve even further we would find another practice that is forbidden in Deuteronomy.

➢ **Offering Prayers to Saints**

Deuteronomy 18:9-12 When thou art come into the land which the LORD thy God giveth thee, thou shalt not learn to do after the abominations of those nations. (10) There shall not be found among you *any one* that maketh his son or his daughter to pass through the fire, *or* that useth divination, *or* an observer of times, or an enchanter, or a witch, (11) Or a charmer, or a consulter with familiar spirits, or a wizard, or a **necromancer**. (12) For all that do these things *are* an abomination unto the LORD: and because of these abominations the LORD thy God doth drive them out from before thee.

The key word here is necromancer. Necromancy, is defined in *Holman's Bible Dictionary* as "Conjuring the spirits of the dead to predict or influence future events."

In the west when we see the word 'conjure' we think of witches sitting around a boiling pot throwing in newt's feet and chanting summons to some spiritual entity. Actually the word conjure simply means **'to charge or entreat solemnly"** . In other words, **to pray to**. So, in effect when a person prays to saints they are committing the sin of necromancy.

All these practices are designed to sway our minds away from Christ and bog it down with religion, man-made traditions and keep our focus on man.

- ➢ We confess our sins to a priest instead of Christ, the HIGH Priest.
- ➢ We are told to do 'penance', as if there were actually something WE can do to remove the sin. (Only Christ and His Blood remove sin) Nothing you do can remove sin!
- ➢ We offer prayers to someone else other than the Father (Father God – Jehovah) knowing that Jesus said to pray to the Father (Jehovah)

These are simply a few of the tenants of orthodoxy that do not line up with scripture. To many, orthodoxy is comfortable. It is simple and all packaged nice and neatly. Simply do whatever the priest tells you to do and you have no worries. Everything is laid into the care of men. Understand that I am not speaking against people, but only against unscriptural practices.

Many other Doctrines of Demons have invaded the church, and I cannot possibly list them all here. What I will leave you with is the best explanation of what we are to be concerned with that is available to us as believers. Paul wrote most of the New Testament. Paul studied at the school of Gamaliel who was considered to be the ultimate teacher of the law, as well as one of the greatest philosophers who ever lived. Paul was the teacher's pet. Paul spoke in his letter to the Philippians about what was truly important and what we are to truly focus on.

Phillipians 3:4-8 Though I might also have confidence in the flesh. If any other man thinketh that he hath whereof he might trust in the flesh, I more: (5) Circumcised the eighth day, of the stock of Israel, *of* the tribe of Benjamin, an Hebrew of the Hebrews; as touching the law, a Pharisee; (6) Concerning zeal, persecuting the church; touching the righteousness which is in the law, blameless.

(7) But what things were gain to me, those I counted loss for Christ. (8) Yea doubtless, and I count all things *but* loss for the excellency of the knowledge of Christ Jesus my Lord: for whom I have suffered the loss of all things, and do count them *but* dung, that I may win Christ,

Note his use of the word dung describing everything else that he could claim. Later in the chapter he gives us the key to focus on.

Philippians 3:9-11 And be found in him, not having mine own righteousness, which is of the law, but that which is through the faith of Christ, the righteousness which is of God by faith: (10) That I may know him, and the power of his resurrection, and the fellowship of his sufferings, being made conformable unto his death; (11) If by any means I might attain unto the resurrection of the dead.

Christ, and Him Crucified.

1Collossians 2:1-4 And I, brethren, when I came to you, came not with excellency of speech or of wisdom, declaring unto you the testimony of God. (2) For I determined not to know any thing among you, save **Jesus Christ, and him crucified.** (3) And I was with you in weakness, and in fear, and in much trembling. (4) And my speech and my preaching *was* not with enticing words of man's wisdom, but in demonstration of the Spirit and of power:

Not fancy words, not fancy mind blowing doctrines. Simply Jesus Christ. Our model is to adopt His cause. What was His cause?
Luke 4:18-19 The Spirit of the Lord *is* upon me, because he hath anointed me to preach the gospel to the poor; he hath sent me to heal the brokenhearted, to preach deliverance to the captives, and recovering of sight to the blind, to set at liberty them that are bruised, (19) To preach the acceptable year of the Lord.

Rather than have a 'purpose driven life' we need a Person Driven Life, built on the Person of Jesus Christ. Any doctrine that deviates from the pure mission of Christ is only going to lead you down a path that will result in loss. We are to adopt the cause of Christ. We are to preach the Gospel. We are to heal, we are to tell people that they can be free, help the blind (spiritually and physically) to recover sight, to set free those who have been oppressed and bruised and to tell them that Jesus is coming.

- To be sidelined into religious practice that is mere tradition of men is loss.
- To be taken away by self fulfilling doctrines of the faith movement and 'new' revelations is loss.
- To be driven like so much chaff in the winds of debate in the face of an agnostic world is loss.
- To be caught up in the pursuit of happiness is loss. Jesus IS our happiness.

Our mission is sure. It is three fold and defined by:
- Preach Christ and Him Crucified.

- Minister to the poor. (Widows and orphans)
- Make disciples of all nations.

Becoming bogged down in anything else is loss.

DOD REDO

Deceptions In Predicting The Rapture

I could not end this critical chapter without including some other points of interest that have had, and seem to continually have people stirred up trying to pin down the rapture. Below I have included several things from the past and some that are presently at the time of this writing causing people to have false hope.

"88"

The first deception about the timing of the rapture that I personally remember occurred in 1988. A book was penned and sold over 300,000 copies with the title '88

Reasons Why The Rapture Will Be In 88". Millions heard the message, or at least a version of it as Pastors preached right from the book in their pulpits. Of course, Jesus did not come in 1988 and unbelievably, the book is still available for purchase.

Generation Timing

Now another current pinpointing scheme is circling in Christian circles. It is based on the information below and Jesus's words that the generation that sees Israel come back to her land will not pass away until all is fulfilled. Understand before reading that I do believe the scripture that this doctrine is based on. I simply know that there are errors in the numbers that this new thinking is using.

"(Rebirth of modern day Israel) **1948 + 70 yr generation=2018**

(re-capturing of the Temple Mount) **1967 + 50 yr Jubilee =2017/2018**

(seven year Tribulation period) **2018-7 yr Tribulation=2011** "

This one would be fine were it not for some critical flaws. A biblical generation is 100 years according to the promise made to Abraham in Genesis:

Genesis 15:13-16 And He said to Abram, You must surely know that your seed shall be a stranger in a land not theirs, and shall serve them. And they shall afflict them **four hundred years**. (14) And also I will judge that nation whom they shall serve. And afterward they shall come out with great substance. (15) And you shall go to your fathers in peace. You shall be buried in a good old age. (16) But in the **fourth generation** they shall come here again, for the iniquity of the Amorites is not yet full.

Four generations = four hundred years. Do the math. That makes each generation 100 years. The plan above uses 70 years as a generation. That is based on a scripture in Psalms that says that the years of a man's life will be 70. Not a generation, but rather the years of a man's life. The second fault is that the Tribulation period is not 7 years. The last week of Daniel's vision is 7 years. The Tribulation only lasts a portion of that 7 year period.

"Comet Elenin"

This teaching snared and entranced countless believers and non believers with the premise that a rogue comet, or as some said a 'brown dwarf star' was entering the galaxy and on the 27th of September, 2011 was going to cause massive solar flares and earthquakes. All this was going to time out with Rosh Hashanah and the blowing of the trumpet. The rapture was to occur somewhere around 2-3AM CST.

It sounded pretty good. A juicy cocktail of end time signs & feast dates, an astronomical calamity of Hollywood proportions, hidden planets, 3 days of darkness on Earth and even the President running to a Colorado bunker to hide out in the middle of the key dates. Something must be up. All the You Tube video makers plotted the course, keeping us alarmed, the watchmen cried out, odd photos circulated, the endless Facebook posts & video shares by many people over the past 6 months all counted down to its climax. Never has a block of dirty ice attracted the attention of so many!!

THE FACTS

The facts are it was a comet, only a few miles in diameter that possessed barely enough gravitational pull to affect anything. It would only come within 25 million miles at its closest point to Earth (90 times further than the moon, similar distance to Venus). Comets have come and gone before without doing anything, and this one was always destined to be a non-event.

THE FALSEHOOD

The following were the major False claims repeatably observed from many people:

- The Comet has already caused many earthquakes and was going to cause destructive mayhem during its sun/earth alignment 26-29 Sept -FALSE

- It was also going to cause an eclipse of 3 days of darkness over the Earth between 26-29 Sept -FALSE

- Hidden behind the Comet was a rogue Planet (Planet X/Nibiru/Brown Dwarf Star) that was really 3 times as big as Jupiter and would cause gravitational mayhem & disasters all over the Earth -FALSE

Many other things were said and 'reported' but these above will suffice for now to show the deception that surrounded this event. We must realize that if we preach and share falsehood we can bring reproach on the name of Christ & cause confusion & distraction to many. It can also lead us to give false witness to disasters that do happen - saying its caused by a comet, rather than as direct judgments for sin.

TRIP ROPES OF DECEPTION

Jesus warned us that in the end times there would be deception. Here are some reasons that we can be deceived:

- We can be deceived by a seemingly **strong line up of events**, especially when we really **want something to happen.** In this case using scriptures of signs in the Heavens that we do expect to see: in the sun, moon and stars as signs of Christ's coming; the Israel feast dates; Palestine at the UN issue at the same time; the testimony of the 'NASA' guy on You Tube and all the other you tube videos; and there was the Nibiru theory which is actually based on New Age teachings. The woman who started this one said she got her Nibiru messages from Aliens.

- We can be deceived even by the **fear of deception**. Many refused to believe the official NASA report on the comet because of general government deception. But in this case even amateur Astronomers who can view it mostly agreed it was just a small comet which was even breaking up as it passed the Sun.
- We can be deceived when **lots of people are jumping on the bandwagon**. Many 'watchmen' & online bible teachers repeated the claims, as did many who read or watch their teachings. Lets be cautious of the buzz of sensationalism & hype, and keep a sound mind.
- We can be deceived if anything gets before a close relationship with the Lord, such as business in ministry, seeking to be first to break a story on FB,

or seeking signs. If we have not regularly come to Him, as He requested, to learn of Him, there will then be a subtle form of pride in our own heart that can cause us to be led astray.

We must always strive to go to the Word of God, NOT to prove our theory to be correct but to simply see what the Spirit will teach us. He will guide us into all truth if we only listen to Him. And as we see the day approaching, we need the guidance of the Spirit more and more.

"In this late hour, prophecy teachers in America have convinced millions of Christians they will never face the Antichrist. According to Jesus, believers should be watching for the invasion of Jerusalem by the Abomination of Desolation before the Son of Man gathers His elect (Luke 21:20-27). Paul also taught the Man of Sin must be revealed before the Lord gathers His elect (2 Thessalonians. 2:1-4). Such respected leaders from the early church, Irenaeus, Justin Martyr, Tertullian, and Hippolytus, taught the Antichrist would war against the saints (Revelation. 13:7). This is why anyone teaching the saints will be raptured first is taking away from the prophecy of Revelation. " *

* Paul Bortolazzo – Til Eternity

Little c Big G

I knew you would be intrigued by the title of this chapter. I hoped that you would not skip ahead. But here you are now and here we go. Little c (church) = Big G (government) is the topic that few want to hear.

Reason? It means that they probably didn't do their job in the Kingdom, and no one wants to hear that they didn't do their job. Especially from the King of Kings.

First, a few facts. I am not a proponent of tithing, but I am a huge proponent of giving. To tithe means you fulfilled what you thought to be your obligation and nothing more. You did enough to 'get your ticket'. But you still feel empty because you only did what you thought was required. That is why I and many others have abandoned tithing in favor of giving. I can give more than what would be my tithe (usually do) and do so with joy, knowing that when I give God will always give back more than I gave.

> ➤ Tithing is the law and flesh. Tithing is obligatory and carnal. Tithing is a requirement that needs to be

fulfilled. Tithing is tradition. Tithing is forever tied to priesthood and the inequality of 'clergy and laity'. Tithing was old covenant.

➢ Giving is Spirit and life. Giving is from the heart. Giving is a sure indicator that the giver has been set free from law and tradition. Giving gives a return that may come not in the manner of monetary gain but most often comes in the form of peace of heart. Giving is the evidence of a soul set free. Giving is new covenant.

However, if you believe that tithing is the way for you to go, hold on as I give you food for thought. If you think that tithing is giving ten percent, you have fallen short. Oh sure, the very word tithe means 'a tenth part' but there may be some things that you are not aware of.

The children of Israel were commanded to give a total of 23.3%. The Mosaic Law required the children of Israel to pay three different tithes:

➢ **Levitical tithe** (Leviticus 27:30-32; Numbers 18:21,24)

> **Annual festival tithe** (Deuteronomy 14:22-27)
> **Tri-annual poor tithe** (Deuteronomy 14:28-29).

The Levitical Tithe was the standard tithe. It required all Israelites to give 10% of their increase (crops, fruit, livestock) to the Levites. This tithe was offered sporadically throughout the year as crops came in and livestock were born.

The Festival Tithe was to be "paid" annually when the Jews gathered in Jerusalem for one of the national festivals. The worshiper was instructed to take an additional 10% of his annual increase to Jerusalem and consume it together with his family and the Levites, at the festival. They feast would consist of grains, meat, and drink.

The Poor Tithe was paid every three years. Like the festival tithe, this tithe was intended to feed others, including Levites. Unlike the festival tithe, however, this tithe was intended to feed **foreigners, orphans, and widows**—not at Jerusalem, but within one's own city. Rather than tithing on the past three years, the worshiper only had to tithe on his increase for the year in which the poor tithe was required. **All this added up to 23.3% annually.**

Now, armed with that thought take a look at how much you pay in taxes on average. In the U.S. The top bracket is 35% and the bottom bracket is 15%. That makes the average according to the population and based on how many are in each bracket **about 23%**. I do NOT think that to be a coincidence. You see, about the time the Church stopped taking care of the poor, the government picked up the task. When did all this come about? I will do like my Hero Jesus and answer that question with a question. About what time frame did the rise of prosperity teaching and the 'faith' movement come into being? The answer is that prosperity theology came into being riding on the coat tails of the great healing crusades of the 1950's. It was only a few years later that the Great Society legislation of the 1960's opened the floodgates for our present welfare system.

Let me give you another take on an old story. Everyone almost has heard of how God destroyed Sodom and Gomorrah. Almost everyone would agree, and has heard it preached and taught that lewdness, perversion and homosexuality were the sins that caused the twin cities to come under judgement. However, the Bible paints a clear picture of the sin that brought their demise in the writings of Ezekiel.

Ezekiel 16:48-50 *As* I live, saith the Lord GOD, Sodom thy sister hath not done, she nor her daughters, as thou hast done, thou and thy daughters. (49) Behold, this was the iniquity of thy sister Sodom, pride, fulness of bread, and abundance of idleness was in her and in her daughters, <u>neither did she strengthen the hand of the poor and needy.</u> (50) And they were haughty, and committed abomination before me: therefore I took them away as I saw *good.*

Sodom's greatest sin was the **neglect of the poor**, coupled with her pride. This is a perfect description of the Western Church today. People attend service at great cathedrals and worship centers across the land and are prideful of their 'church' to the point of telling others how much better theirs is than the one down the road. Couple that with giving to keep the doors of that huge edifice open as opposed to giving to the poor and you have a similar setup as was in Sodom. There were church folk in Sodom. Lot was there and was a righteous man, but had grown complacent to all that was surrounding him even to the point of saying nothing about it. There are church folk here in the western culture but we have turned inward and are concerned with sustaining our lifestyle at the expense of the poor. God help us. Below is a time-line that helps you to understand.

The Church grew inward as people began giving to various ministries that promised that God would bless those who gave. Giving to the poor went out the window when promoting huge TV and Radio ministries became popular instead. So, the inroads of little church – big government slowly crept in. As a consequence:

In the **1960's** we lost the right to pray in a public school. We kept sowing seed into the faith movement and big ministries in the hopes that our own pockets would swell, and also that these ministries would collectively fulfill our obligations while we went about with our lifestyles of 'getting more'.

In the **1970's** we began paying more and more taxes and government grew and grew. And we started paying ministers salaries in the six figure range as mega-churches began to spring up. And the church grew more and more inward. Our obligation was no longer to the poor but to feed the machine we know as 'church'. Great swelling sermons were preached on tithing ten percent to maintain what had been built. Building size grew as control freaks hiding in the office of pastor silently refused to allow the Head of the church (Jesus) to be the head. As long as people were entertained and tradition was preserved we were alright. And the poor were forgotten and government grew.

In the **1980's** various mega ministry leaders fell to sin and we simply found others to give to. We talked in disgust about the leaders who had disgraced 'us' and poured our money into 'Christian Television'. As the communication age with personal computers and cell phones took hold the church grew more and more inward while professing that technology was going to help proclaim the Gospel all over the world and usher in Jesus's return. We pumped in the money and forgot the poor. And we talked about how bad our politicians were and how high taxes were. And government grew even more.

In the **1990's** the payroll of the federal government made it the single greatest employer in the world and the church swooned after new messages about how we could have our best life in the here and now. The great majority of believers were more concerned with what God could do for them, than what they could do for God. And the poor were forgotten and government grew bigger.

The **2000's** saw ministers with fleets of corporate jets, all paid for by the church, and government continued to grow. Like a group of money hungry converts at a multi-level marketing conference, we flocked to hear the latest heresy from popular faith movement teachers. We became bogged down in self help conferences that did nothing more than line the pockets of the teachers. The divorce rate in the church was even with the non church world. We pumped in our money on books that promised 12 steps to this, or that. And we were even more empty than before. The poor were forgotten and government grew, and we complained.

Now in the **2010's** we dare to complain about how government is beginning to intrude into our lives and privacy. Church of the Living God, wake up! We did it to ourselves. What the church failed to do was simply picked up by the government.

I look and compare the rise and fall of Rome and the United States to the rise and fall of the Western Church. There are a lot of similarities, so I offer you the preamble to the fall of the Western Church. It is loosely based on the preamble to the Constitution of the United States.

The Preamble To The Fall Of The Western Church
We the people of the Western Church, in order to form a more perfect worship service, establish our denomination as better than the others , insure everyone has a blessed day, provide for the comfort of our pastor and staff, promote the next great building fund drive, and secure the blessings of Jabez to ourselves and our college fund for our kids, do ordain and establish this Doctrine Of Prosperity for the Church with someone else's name on the marquee.

Government was allowed to become huge and intrusive by the Church. It is our fault for not fulfilling our responsibilities to the widows and the orphans and the poor. WE made the decision to turn our heads and let the government do our job, yet we cry every year at tax time. And because we allowed the government to take over social programs that are the responsibility of the church, WE opened the floodgates for more and more control over us in all other areas of our lives.

We have met the enemy and the enemy is us.

No Other Gods

Exodus 20:1-7 And God spake all these words, saying, (2) I *am* the LORD thy God, which have brought thee out of the land of Egypt, out of the house of bondage. (3) Thou shalt have **no other gods** before me. (4) Thou shalt not make unto thee any graven image, or any likeness *of any thing* that *is* in heaven above, or that *is* in the earth beneath, or that *is* in the water under the earth:

I want to share something with you that the Holy Spirit illuminated to me one day. I was pondering the verses above and got a real eye opener. For a moment, lets take it for granted that everyone knows that the verses above are the beginning of the Ten Commandments. Now God has never backed off of the ten commandments, irregardless of what you may think. He is the "same, yesterday, today and forever". He has never once liberalized His covenants with man. He has never once diminished His laws. He has never once changed His mind about His principles, precepts and standards. "I change not" means I change not. Even Jesus summed the ten commandments up by saying that there were two, Love God with all your heart, soul, mind and strength, and love your neighbor as yourself. "All the Law and the Prophets hang on those two", which encompass ALL.

Most people believe that the verses above refer to making some sort of carved, cast, or molded figure and then bowing down to it. And they are correct in that assumption. But with God and His Word there is usually always a spiritual and a physical meaning. The physical would be the images mentioned above that you can see with your physical eyes, created by the hands of man. But I want to share something with you that goes beyond what you create with your hands or see with your eyes. The Holy Spirit showed me in an instant that we have the ability to create spiritual things with our minds also! We have the ability to create our own god that no one can see with the eye. And when we do that, most times the god we create is made in our image, beholding to our standards, principles and precepts.

From this point on in this chapter when I refer to the God of the Holy Bible, that Abraham, Isaac and Jacob worshiped I will call Him Jehovah. This is so you will completely understand which God I am speaking about. (There are many gods that people refer to as God)

Let me give you an example to ponder. Students of the Bible know that God (Jehovah, Yahweh, Elohim, I AM) said in His Word (Bible) that you 'Shall Not Steal'. That one is pretty plain and straightforward. You are not supposed to take anything that belongs to anyone else. To do so is stealing. I mean how simple can that be? But yet there are believers every year that cheat on taxes. That is a form of stealing. There are believers who conduct personal business on company time without permission. That is stealing.

But when approached with the subject of stealing, the justification begins. "Well, I really don't think God would think of that as stealing". "It is only a few minutes". "Everyone here does it". We as humans love to justify our sins. But let's just how far we can take that justification of our own personal beliefs.

How many people do you know that literally believe that when any one of their family members die that they sprout angel wings and are now 'looking down on us, watching out for us'? Go ahead and raise your hand for I assure you that you know someone like this. This ties in with the mindset that Jehovah would surely not send anyone to hell. But in reality there is no scripture to back up this belief. It is simply what they want to believe and the god that they serve surely allows it to be so. So they are no longer serving or referring to Jehovah.

Then there are those who believe that all faiths worship the same God. They say that the Muslim god is the same god because Judaism and Islam are both considered 'Abrahamic' religions. I assure you that Muslims do not worship Jehovah. Buddhists do not worship Jehovah. Hindus, Mormons, and all the rest do not worship Jehovah. But the movement today among many religious leaders is directed towards having you believe that there is only one God and all faiths and religions are working towards the same goal. I assure you they are not.

This doctrine falls in line with another doctrine that says "As long as I am good enough, surely God will let me in". This doctrine negates the work of Christ on the cross and says that He didn't have to die, I can do it by my own goodness. If that were the case, Jesus would not have come. You cannot be good enough on your own. And your own goodness cannot be added to what Jesus did on the cross to somehow make you more acceptable to Jehovah.

What all of this amounts to is recreating Jehovah in YOUR image. In other words, taking Jehovah and saying that He will and won't do this or that based on your personal beliefs. You have now created a new god and his name is not Jehovah. So, you simply call him the generic term of 'god'.

Bear with me as I go further. Jehovah does not change. He does not repent. If he hates thievery in the Old Testament, He hates it now. And if you are a thief and stand before Him one day and have not repented, he has no recourse but to use justice and send you to Hades.

I lost count a long time ago of the times I have heard this next statement: "The god I serve would not do _____ or

_____!" Or, "The god I serve is like _____ or _____." (Fill in the blanks) Here is one of the worst. "There are many paths to god. Jesus is only one of them." Think about what is happening when statements like these are made. You are creating a different god than Jehovah. When you stand before Jehovah and He says "I do not know you", will your defense on that day be something along these lines. "But I prayed to you and worshiped you!" At that point His reply may be along these lines, "No, that was the god you created. I am not like him at all." Understand that Jehovah **does not change**. Just because you feel that tax evasion is not stealing, does not make it so. Jehovah's law is law. Just because you feel that Jehovah would not send people to Hades who had never heard about Jesus, does not require Him to be like that.

Just because you feel that homosexuality is OK, does not mean Jehovah says it is. And when you pray to your god that believes homosexuality is OK, I assure you that you are praying to a creation of your own mind. You are not praying to Jehovah. Jehovah said all through the Bible that homosexuality was a sin.

Leviticus 18:22 Thou shalt not lie with mankind, as with womankind: it *is* abomination.

Leviticus 20:13 If a man also lie with mankind, as he lieth with a woman, both of them have committed an abomination: they shall surely be put to death; their blood *shall be* upon them.

Romans 1:26-28 For this cause God gave them up unto vile affections: for even their women did change the natural use into that which is against nature: (27) And likewise also the men, leaving the natural use of the woman, burned in their lust one toward another; men with men working that which is unseemly, and receiving in themselves that recompense of their error which was meet. (28) And even as they did not like to retain God in *their* knowledge, God gave them over to a reprobate mind, to do those things which are not convenient;

Here are three of numerous passages that give clear direction to the abomination of homosexuality. Every time the bible refers to 'Sodomites', that is a direct reflection to the sin that had permeated Sodom and Gomorrah. So if your god will allow homosexuals to enter into Heaven, then your god is not Jehovah.

The process of creating our own gods has been going on since Adam, Eve and the garden. Following those gods has been detrimental to the fulfillment of the Great Commission, for one of the most dangerous gods out there is the god that allows you to not witness about Jesus. This is the god that allows you to say "I'm not going to bother anyone about their faith. As long as they are happy with it, who am I to tell them they need to change?" This is the same god that All religions point to, the one that 'We are all working to get to'. This is not Jehovah, who tells us to go forth and make disciples of all nations.

A classic, and perhaps one the most powerful examples of creating another god in our own image is the Jefferson Bible. Almost everyone has heard of one of the founding fathers of the United States, Thomas Jefferson. Jefferson set about to take the Gospels of Matthew, Mark, Luke and John and effectively edit them to form his own bible. Using a razor, Jefferson actually cut and arranged selected verses from the four books in chronological order, mingling excerpts from one text to those of another in order to create a single narrative. He omitted any references to the Deity of Christ, as well as anything supernatural such as healings. What he ended up with was his own gospel that was subtitled 'The Life And Morals Of Jesus Of Nazareth'. His narrative ends with the stone being rolled over the tomb. In his book, Jesus never resurrected.

It is far too easy for us to create not only our own god, but also dictate how he will dance. And we wonder why Jehovah is about to unleash His wrath on this sin sick world.

Section II

OK, I Understand

Lets talk for a moment, now that you have read through the short story and agree that indeed 'All Hell' has broken loose and the 'Pre-Tribulation Rapture' did not happen. You have read the chapters following and now understand why God is angry and You have not taken the mark of the beast (or it has not started yet). And you want to be ready but are not sure what you need to be ready for. This second part is designed to help you prepare for the harsh times ahead. We begin with a crash course in events that you should be on the watch for, if they have not already taken place by the time you read this book.

A Crash Course

My great friend Paul Bortolazzo is an important adviser to me concerning Eschatology. His book Til Eternity is a primer for any student of End Time Events. I asked his permission to borrow and steal from Til Eternity. He graciously agreed to let me quote and I am grateful, not for my sake but for YOUR sake so that you will be able to see the truth and be prepared. Anything you read in this chapter that is in both ***italics and bold type*** is a direct quote from Til Eternity.

In 1976 I was born again in a radical fashion from a life of addiction. God has kept me since that day and I owe everything to Him. That first year of my new life in Christ I read the entire Bible through at least four times. I also read The Revelation Of Jesus Christ no less than 60 times. I simply could not put my Bible down. I was now an addict to the Word of God.

In my first book Walking Backwards I included a chapter entitled 'There Be Giants'. In that chapter I relay a tale of how I began to see the truth of the 6th Seal rapture early in my walk with Christ. I began to question teachers and preachers who taught Pre-Tribulation Rapture. I soon found that I was fighting a battle that I could not win in my own strength and in the time frame I chose. God is my strength and He also has His own timetable. I could not face the giant of established teachers until due time, and until He said to do so. So I held the truth for many years, sharing with whoever would listen in a discreet manner. Remember in his letter to the church at Corinth Paul said that "The spirit of the prophet is subject to the prophet". This means that if what you have been given to speak from God is true, you will be able to hold it until the right time to speak it forth. So, I bid my time and waited. Then God sent Paul Bortolazzo to me via a Wednesday evening service in the church where I was serving as music minister. That night as he began to teach and got to the 6th Seal and declared what I had seen years before, I thanked God for His provision of a brother who not only understood but would not compromise. Since then Paul has written Til Eternity and also a novel trilogy based on End Time events entitled The Coming.

Below in bullet format is a step by step set of events that you need to be aware of to be prepared for the persecution to come, or that may already be here. This is a digested list of which the full meat is contained within Til Eternity. In Paul's book He outlines the 70 distinct events of End Time Prophecy. I take a few liberties to list what I perceive to be the events you should look for that will be manifested here on earth for the visible eye to see. These events are in Chronological order so that you will be aware of what you need to know to be looking for. Remember, some of these events may have happened before you got your hands on this book! As of this writing in the Fall of 2011 they have not occurred yet.

> **The Signing of a Peace Accord** between Israel and her surrounding neighbors. (Daniel 9:27) This event signals the **beginning** of the final week of Daniel's 70 week vision. 69 weeks of the vision have been fulfilled and one week (7 years) is left. Some incorrectly refer to this period as the Tribulation period. That is an erroneous doctrine. Tribulation only occurs for a period of time within the 7 years that are the final week. Before

Tribulation you will have what Jesus declared to be the 'Beginning of Sorrows'.

- **The 1st Seal is broken in Heaven**. (Revelation 6:2) There is a scroll in heaven with 7 Seals. The only one found worthy to open the scroll is the Lamb of God (Jesus). When He opens the 1st Seal the earth is in biblical terms 'conquered'. This is manifested in the physical world but is rooted and driven by the spirit realm. Once great nations now are broken and begin lining up to follow a world leader. He is the same man who will 'broker' the peace accord between Israel and her Muslim neighbors.

- **The 2nd Seal is broken in heaven**. (Revelation 6:4) Men begin to kill each other as never before. *"The Lord doesn't tell us how many nations will be involved in these wars (Luke 21:9-10). We aren't told how many people will die. We do know that Israel will be at peace during this time."*

- **The 3rd Seal is broken in Heaven**. Total, Worldwide economic collapse ensues. (Revelation 6:5-6) *"After the opening of the 3rd seal, a daily* *wage won't be able to buy much food. While on the Mount of Olives Jesus exhorts His elect to watch for famines, pestilences, and earthquakes."*... And there will be famines, pestilences, and earthquakes in various places. All these are the beginning of sorrows." (Matthew. 24:7-8) *"The Lord calls these events the beginning of sorrows. The events in Matthew 24:4-7 are the same events John saw after the opening of the first three seals in Revelation 6:1-6. Satan is going to manipulate teachers coming in Christ's name to deceive many (Matthew. 24:4-5). Christians who once believed in sound doctrine are going to be duped by the sincerity and passion of these teachers.* " At the time of this writing there is economic distress like I have never seen in my lifetime, but it cannot compare to the collapse that will help to user in the System of the Beast.

- **War In Heaven**. You won't see this one, but trust me when I say that you will be affected by this. Michael the great Archangel and his angels will cast Satan out of Heaven for the last time. Satan will come to earth filled with anger. The persecution of the believers will begin. This is NOT the wrath of God, remember that this is the wrath of Satan. Revelation Chapter 12 is the documentation of this event. Don't worry that chapter 12 is after chapters 6-8 where the seals are being broken. Not everything in Revelation is is chronological order.

- **The 4th Seal is broken in Heaven.** (Revelation 6:8) The rider of the pale horse goes forth and ¼ (One Fourth- 25%) of the world population is killed by 'the sword', hunger, death and beasts of the earth. Many of these who are killed are believers who refuse to take the Mark.
- **Tribulation.** Satan makes war with the saints. This is in conjunction with the 4th seal being broken. *"John is in the Spirit before the throne of God. The 144,000 are being protected in the wilderness (Revelation 12:6). Satan has been cast out of heaven and Michael the restrainer has been taken out of the way (Revelation 12:7-12, 2 Thessalonians 2:7, Daniel12:1). The beginning of*

sorrows is over." Note that the beginning of sorrows is done at this point. Now comes the wrath of Satan against believers. This is tribulation, not the Wrath of God against those who will worship the beast. Please also understand the meaning of worshiping the beast. This does not mean holding a church service and praying to him. Worship is in this context veneration of the beast and his system, which culminates in the ultimate act of homage by taking his mark on your body.

- **The Beast.** (Revelation 13:11) The Abomination of Desolation. The wicked one. The man who directed the peace accord. The man that the whole world marveled at and follows. He commands everyone to take a mark in order to buy and sell. To take this mark removes your name from the Book of Life. All nations will fall behind him and his plan. We are not told how long it will take to mark everyone.

- **The Two Witnesses.** Appearing from seemingly nowhere, they begin to preach against the beast. They are supernaturally protected by God. They can call down fire from Heaven and hold back rain.

- **The 1ˢᵗ Angel** flies through the heavens proclaiming the Gospel.
- **2ⁿᵈ Angel proclaims that 'Mystery Babylon' has fallen.** Mystery Babylon is the unified worldwide religion that the beast uses to usher in worship of himself. Now Satan has no more use for this system now that people are effectively worshiping the beast. This religious system is a combination of all faiths supposedly working together for world peace. Even now at this writing we see the groundwork being laid through false teaching within the church. Great teachers of the Christian faith are being used to usher in this system and do not have a clue that the heresy they preach is the very thing that will cause believers to fall and take the mark of the beast.
- **3ʳᵈ Angel** warns people to not worship the beast.
- **The Great Falling Away,** as believers give in to the system and deny Christ. As stated before, this is due to false teaching that plays down the terrible circumstances of taking the mark. Too much importance is placed on this life, and too little

placed on our life in eternity. Too much teaching is centered on how to prosper now with no thought on the hereafter. Also, the heresy of OSAS (once saved always saved) plays into this by having believers think that they cannot lose their salvation. Remember, most believers HAVE NOT studied these things for themselves and simply go along with the doctrines spewed forth from pulpits. The deception will be convincing and many will fall from faith, all the while believing that their salvation is secure.

- **The 5th Seal is broken in Heaven**. The persecution of those who follow Jesus and refuse to take the mark of the beast culminates in the appearance of souls who had been martyred during the Tribulation. (Revelation 6:9-11) The bible declares that they are 'under the altar' and are waiting on the Resurrection (Rapture), and waiting on God to avenge their deaths on the beast. Many will lose their earthly life rather than take the mark. (They loved not their lives, even unto death)

> **The 6th Seal is broken in Heaven.** (Revelation 6:12 – 8:1) The following events happen after the 6th Seal is broken.

1. A GREAT earthquake like known history has never experienced. (See #5)
2. The Sun Darkens. Described as sackcloth in the Bible. This signifies that the light will barely be enough to see by. This has happened once before, when Christ hung on the cross.
3. The Moon turns red as blood. Of course this is a direct reflection of the Sun being darkened.
4. The Stars fall. Even the heavens are misplaced as Christ comes in power to gather His elect.
5. **Every** mountain and island are moved. Every one. The great earthquake in #1 is of such a significant power that the entire world is affected by it.
6. The winds of the earth are stopped by four great angels. No wind blows. None.
7. The sign of His coming is visible, like lightning from one end of the sky to the other, all over the world.

8. A great Trumpet is blown.
9. Jesus appears in the clouds. (Matthew 24:30)
10. Angels are dispatched to gather the Elect (Matthew 24:31)
11. A great multitude dressed in white suddenly 'appears' in Heaven. (The rapture has occurred) Revelation 7:9

➤ **The 7th Seal is broken in Heaven**, and there is Silence in Heaven for a half hour. (Revelation 8:1) NOW begins the **Wrath of God.** Understand that there has never been silence in Heaven before. If nothing else, there are special angels who fly around the throne day and night singing Holy Holy Holy. Even they stop for a half hour to ponder the significance of what is about to happen. Wrath is about to be poured out on the wicked who have been left behind. Also understand the use of the word wicked. This does not mean only criminals and lewd, mean people. This can mean ANYONE who has not allowed Christ into their heart – no matter how good they live their lives!

Study this time-line above. Know that there are perilous times for believers ahead (Depending on when you read this) in which you will have to make choices that may cost your very life. You will either take the mark of the beast, or you will not be able to buy or sell. Please understand that the very systems that are in place at this writing (2011) are designed to cause you to compromise your faith in Christ. You are being bombarded with political correctness and asked to go along with the belief that all religions lead to God.

The deception is smooth and great. Swelling words by skillful orators who have graced pulpits and TV and radio will have you believing the following:

- **Nothing in prophecy has to be fulfilled before the rapture.**
- **Jesus could come at any moment without any notice.** If this is true then Jesus himself was wrong in Matthew 24:27-30 when he gives the same signs of the 4th seal concerning Sun, Moon and His sign in the clouds.
- Jesus also said in Matthew to 'watch and pray'. The deceivers will tell you that He was **speaking to**

Jews. Do not believe them. Your salvation may depend on what you believe, for if the Pre-Trib rapture does not occur as you have believed, then you may end up with your faith shipwrecked.

Once the rapture has plainly past the 'Pre-trib' point in time there will most likely be denial and a change of preaching. They will still believe that God will not allow anything bad to happen. This will lead to the following:

➢ Advising you that this simple little tattoo cannot be the mark and it will be alright. (I am assuming that it may be some form of organic tattoo (invisible).

➢ Advising you that you will not lose your place in heaven if you take the mark. (Further denial)

Here are the three events that believers **will see** during Daniel's 70th Week:

➢ The Signing of the Peace Accord by the Man of Sin (begins Daniel's "Week of Seven Years," called the "beginning of sorrows")

➢ The Abomination of Desolation Standing in the Holy Place (in the "Middle of the Week," three and a half years after the signing of the Covenant).

- ➤ The Sign of the Son of Man in the Heavens (the Resurrection of the Dead and the Rapture of the Church) sometime between when the 6th and the 7th Seal is opened.

The deceptions will be great, but subtle. A great friend of mine has a mother who lived in Germany during WWII. I assure you that the German populace had no idea what was happening to the Jews. It was only after it was revealed that they began to know and the indoctrination was subtle and great. This lady was a little girl when one day she was standing by the railroad tracks. A train loaded with prisoners came by and she was shocked at the condition that these civilians were being subjected to. She ran home to tell her parents and they thought she was crazy. They had been exposed to the heavily censored and cleverly doctored propaganda and never saw the horror coming.

Don't be fooled. Believers who are alive at the end times will suffer persecution. It will NOT be the wrath of a loving God. That will come later after believers are taken out to be with their Lord.

"Persecution will begin after the Beast seizes authority over the nations (Matthew 24:15, 2 Thessalonians 2:3-4, Rev. 13:5-7). The False Prophet will force the world to worship this man (Revelation 13:11-18). No one will be allowed to buy or sell without receiving his mark on their right hand or forehead. We aren't told how long it will take to mark those on the earth. We do know the worship of the Beast must begin in the second half of the 70th week; between the opening of the 4th and 5th seals (Rev. 6:9-11) Everyone overcoming the Beast during the Great Tribulation will be blessed as their works follow them to heaven (Revelation 14:12-13). Jesus promises to never blot their names out of the Book of Life (Revelation 3:5). Anyone worshiping the Beast will be doomed to the lake of fire (Revelation 13:13-18; 14:9-11; 20:10-15). Their torment will be forever and ever."

Now WHat?

Straightforward talk is the answer to that question. Mary Poppins sang "A Spoonful Of Sugar Helps The Medicine Go Down" and the children were better able to swallow their cough syrup. I'm not sure if sugar would help the medicine of the truth in this book go down well. All I can do is help you understand what you must do, and I pray that my words are inspired by the Holy Spirit to help you become an overcomer.

What do I do now that I am 'in the thick of it all' and am not sure which way to turn? That is a question that will haunt you for some time. Most likely you prepared nothing to help you be self sufficient. Most likely you still are dependent on power, water and all the comforts of a system that has now gone awry since the economy has tanked and whole municipalities are bankrupt. You haven't a clue how to purify water. If you can't buy it in the store, you have no idea how to cook it. If so, you will have pressure on you to simply live and may give in to the mark in order to simply live. I pray not. I pray that God directs you to one of the people who is mentioned in the next paragraph.

Or perhaps you are the type who has the skills needed to survive apocalyptic scenarios. I assure you that if you have been a 'follower' for the majority of your life, you will now become a leader as others who are not prepared come to depend on you. This is your time to be of a great help knowing that God has prepared you for such a time as this. You may well be one of the people who will assist those who wish to bug-out to escape persecution after the mark is instituted.

The Single Most Important Thing Right Now

The single most important thing to consider at this point is just how valuable your earthly life is to you. Is your treasure laid up in Heaven or is it here on earth? This question might very well arise and will have to be answered in the days to come. You may find yourself in a situation that will cause you to "choose this day who you will serve" even to the point of giving up your earthly life.

Another possibility is perhaps God is calling you to be like Rick in the short story. You may be one that He is calling to live within a breath of earthly death. Every moment of your life here will be lived in an underground fashion once the Beast system takes full control. But your mission will be to assist those who were not prepared.
I am here to let you know that God is well able to protect you until the day of the rapture, and He is equally well able to give you the grace to face possible martyrdom.

Corrie Ten Boom

Corrie lived through the Nazi death camps in WWII. Her family was not Jewish, but rather had compassion on Jews even to the point of hiding them. They were caught doing so and were given over to suffering along with the Jews. In 1974 she wrote a letter concerning the coming persecution and tribulation that will soon take over the Christians of this age. I have taken only a few liberties with her letter such as putting some points in bullets, bold font, etc. The letter in it's entirety is here below.

Corrie's Letter

The world is deathly ill. It is dying. The Great Physician has already signed the death certificate. Yet there is still a great work for Christians to do. They are to be streams of living water, channels of mercy to those who are still in the world. It is possible for them to do this because they are overcomers.

Christians are ambassadors for Christ. They are representatives from Heaven to this dying world. And because of our presence here, things will change.

My sister, Betsy, and I were in the Nazi concentration camp at Ravensbruck because we committed the crime of loving Jews. Seven hundred of us from Holland, France, Russia, Poland and Belgium were herded into a room built for two hundred. As far as I knew, Betsy and I were the **only two representatives of Heaven** in that room.

We may have been the Lord's only representatives in that place of hatred, yet because of our presence there, things changed. Jesus said, "In the world you shall have tribulation; but be of good cheer, I have overcome the world." We too, are to be overcomers—bringing the light of Jesus into a world filled with darkness and hate.

Sometimes I get frightened as I read the Bible, and as I look in this world and see all of the tribulation and persecution promised by the Bible coming true. Now I can tell you, though, if you too are afraid, that I have just read the last pages. I can now come to shouting "Hallelujah! Hallelujah!" for I have found where it is written that Jesus said, "He that overcometh shall inherit all things: and I will be His God, and he shall be My son."

This is the future and hope of this world. Not that the world will survive – but that we shall be overcomers in the midst of a dying world.

Betsy and I, in the concentration camp, prayed that God would heal Betsy who was so weak and sick. "Yes, the Lord will heal me," Betsy said with confidence. She died the next day and I could not understand it. They laid her thin body on the concrete floor along with all the other corpses of the women who died that day.

It was hard for me to understand, to believe that God had a purpose for all that. Yet because of Betsy's death, today

I am traveling all over the world telling people about Jesus.

There are some among us teaching there will be no tribulation, that the Christians will be able to escape all this. These are the **false teachers** that Jesus was warning us to expect in the latter days. Most of them have little knowledge of what is already going on across the world. I have been in countries where the saints are already suffering terrible persecution. In China, the Christians were told, "Don't worry, before the tribulation comes you will be translated – raptured." Then came a terrible persecution. Millions of Christians were tortured to death. Later I heard a Bishop from China say, sadly, "We have failed. We should have made the people strong for persecution rather than telling them Jesus would come first. Tell the people how to be strong in times of persecution, how to stand when the tribulation comes – to stand and not faint."

I feel I have a divine mandate to go and tell the people of this world that it is possible to be strong in the Lord Jesus Christ. We are in training for the tribulation, but more than sixty percent of the Body of Christ across the world has already entered into the tribulation. There is no way to escape it. **We are next.**

Since I have already gone through prison for Jesus' sake, and since I met the Bishop in China, now every time I read a good Bible text I think, "Hey, I can use that in the time of tribulation." Then I write it down and learn it by heart.

When I was in the concentration camp, a camp where only twenty percent of the women came out alive, we tried to cheer each other up by saying, "Nothing could be any worse than today." But we would find the next day was even worse. During this time a Bible verse that I had committed to memory gave me great hope and joy. "If ye be reproached for the name of Christ, happy are ye; for the spirit of glory and of God resteth upon you; on their part evil is spoken of, but on your part He is glorified." (I Peter 3:14) I found myself saying, "Hallelujah! Because I am suffering, Jesus is glorified!"

In America, the churches sing, "Let the congregation escape tribulation," but in China and Africa the tribulation has already arrived. This last year alone more than two hundred thousand Christians were martyred in Africa.

Now things like that never get into the newspapers because they cause bad political relations. But I know. I have been there. We need to think about that when we sit down in our nice houses with our nice clothes to eat our steak dinners. Many, many members of the Body of Christ are being tortured to death at this very moment, yet we continue right on as though we are all going to escape the tribulation.

Several years ago I was in Africa in a nation where a new government had come into power. The first night I was there some of the Christians were commanded to come to the police station to register. When they arrived they were arrested and that same night they were executed. The next day the same thing happened with other Christians. The third day it was the same. All the Christians in the district were being systematically murdered.

The fourth day I was to speak in a little church. The people came, but they were filled with fear and tension. All during the service they were looking at each other, their eyes asking, "Will this one I am sitting beside be the next one killed? Will I be the next one?"

The room was hot and stuffy with insects that came through the screen-less windows and swirled around the naked bulbs over the bare wooden benches. I told them a story out of my childhood.

"When I was a little girl, " I said, "I went to my father and said, "Daddy, I am afraid that I will never be strong enough to be a martyr for Jesus Christ." "Tell me," said Father, "When you take a train trip to Amsterdam, when do I give you the money for the ticket? Three weeks before?" "No, Daddy, you give me the money for the ticket just before we get on the train." "That is right," my father said, "and so it is with God's strength. Our Father in Heaven knows when you will need the strength to be a martyr for Jesus Christ. He will supply all you need—just in time…"

My African friends were nodding and smiling. Suddenly a spirit of joy descended upon that church and the people began singing, " In the sweet, by and by, we shall meet on that beautiful shore." Later that week, half the congregation of that church was executed. I heard later that the other half was killed some months ago.

But I must tell you something. I was so happy that the Lord used me to encourage these people, for unlike many of their leaders, I had the word of God. I had been to the Bible and discovered that Jesus said He had not only overcome the world, but to all those who remained faithful to the end, He would give a crown of life.

How can we get ready for the persecution?

- ➤ First we need to feed on the word of God, digest it, make it a part of our being. This will mean disciplined Bible study each day as we not only memorize long passages of scripture, but put the principles to work in our lives.

- ➤ Next we need to develop a personal relationship with Jesus Christ. Not just the Jesus of yesterday, the Jesus of History, but the life-changing Jesus of today who is still alive and sitting at the right hand of God.

- We must be filled with the Holy Spirit. This is no optional command of the Bible, it is absolutely necessary. Those earthly disciples could never have stood up under the persecution of the Jews and Romans had they not waited for Pentecost. Each of us needs our own personal Pentecost, the baptism of the Holy Spirit. We will never be able to stand in the tribulation without it.

- In the coming persecution we must be ready to help each other and encourage each other. But we must not wait until the tribulation comes before starting. The fruit of the Spirit should be the dominant force of every Christian's life.

Many are fearful of the coming tribulation, they want to run. I, too, am a little bit afraid when I think that after all my eighty years, including the horrible Nazi concentration camp, that I might have to go through the tribulation also. But then I read the Bible and I am glad.

When I am weak, then I shall be strong, the Bible says. Betsy and I were prisoners for the Lord; we were so weak, but we got power because the Holy Spirit was on us. That mighty inner strengthening of the Holy Spirit helped us through. No, you will not be strong in yourself when the tribulation comes. Rather, you will be strong in the power of Him who will not forsake you. For seventy-six years I have known the Lord Jesus and not once has He ever left me, or let me down. Though He slay me, yet will I trust Him, for I know that to all who overcome, He shall give the crown of life. Hallelujah!

(End of Letter)

Corrie went to Jesus on April 15th, 1983, but her words are truth. She was a sincere watchman for the Lord, echoing His directives for all believers to 'watch and pray'. The truths enclosed in Corrie's letter are simple.

- ➢ Read the Bible. Without the living Word of God residing in your heart, you will surely fall to the pressures of persecution.

2 Timothy 2:15 "Study earnestly to present yourself approved to God, a workman that does not need to be ashamed, rightly dividing the Word of Truth."

- Develop your personal relationship with Jesus. Not religion, not denomination. Not doctrine nor theology. Your relationship with Christ. There is only one way and that is through prayer and reading HIS Word.

- Be filled with the Holy Spirit. This command of Jesus is to all believers. Do not be fooled by false teaching that says the Baptism of the Spirit was only for the apostles, or the first century church. You will need the power of the Holy Spirit to get y9ou through perilous times.

- Be the believer that God called you to be through works and helps. Be the Church. Reach out to others and begin even now to give of yourself.

Let Me Tell You God has led me across many paths while writing this book. And I have incurred many great testimonies from overcoming saints while walking those paths. In Revelation 12:11 the Bible says **"And they overcame him by the blood of the Lamb, and by the word of their testimony; and they loved not their lives unto the death."** I have often taught and preached that there are only two things that no one will be able to debate with you.

The Blood and your own Personal Testimony.

No one can take either from you. You are in charge and no one can refute what God has done for you, personally. Your testimony is a powerful witness for Christ. Below I have gathered many relating to this book and have included with permission from the people who wrote them. I know that they will encourage you as they did me, and will help you to know that God is more than able to get you through anything you must endure!

Kathy wrote:

"Mike, it breaks my heart also that believers refuse to even consider their previous beliefs to be in error. Some of them are family and close friends of mine. I just keep praying earnestly that the Holy Spirit will speak to their spirits to lead them into the truth. I was so in the dark also, before being added to this site in early July. At first I didn't like what I was reading, but somehow the Holy Spirit reached me one day with the frightening truth that I would some day, if I lived that long, face the antichrist. It was one of the most shocking moments of my life, and one that lead to true repentance from being caught up in living for myself. And to think 3 months ago I was one of them, lost in harvesting Farmville crops and feeding imaginary pets. Then the 2 x 4 was applied to the side of my head and life has become so different for me. Now all I want to do is press closer to Jesus and follow the leading of the Holy Spirit. At times in my life I wanted to follow Him, but just never could seem to do so in my own power. Now I'm just leaving it to Him to work it all out. Take me and mold me as you will, not as I will. What seemed so hard before seems so effortless now...just let Him be in control. **Now I am fully surrendered to His will for my life, whatever that entails.** The Holy Spirit is the only One that can work miracles in a person's life. We can encourage others to see the truth, but they must be open to the truth. Need to pray much and share as the Lord leads."

Diana wrote:

"When I am faced with these Pre Tribbers, I merely tell them that if you think that Jesus will not allow you to die for him, what about all the Christians right now, every 3-5 minutes who are being martyred around the world? Are they foolish, because they won't deny Christ. What makes you special, because you live in America? They never have an answer to that. Then I remind them that are not two sets of Christians. One set getting saved before the Great Tribulation and another set getting saved (without the Holy Spirit) after the Great Tribulation begins. Because it is very clear when Jesus said, THE DEAD IN

CHRIST ARE RAPTURED FIRST! THEN WE WHICH ARE ALIVE WILL BE CAUGHT UP TOGETHER WITH THEM! If this **made up** second group of Christians were possible, it would require a second Rapture. The Word Rapture is really Resurrection and there are only TWO. THE RESURRECTION OF THE JUST and THE RESURRECTION OF THE DAMNED happening after the Millennium. This makes them think. I've had Pastors get chocked up on that one. Then they say, "Oh, I am a Pan Trib, whatever pans out!" Like it doesn't matter what the Lord is trying to warn us about. The compromise in the Church today is disgusting. Hey, the Church needs the Tribulation, because they are so lukewarm!"

I understand Diana's situation. I know many who use the Pan-Trib excuse to 'be neutral' on the subject. Jesus told us to watch and pray, not to be neutral. Being neutral is the same thing as sitting on the fence, or being lukewarm in that area. A little leaven leavens the whole loaf. Eventually as compromise is struck in one area, other areas begin to fall short and soon the entire loaf of your life is a compromise.

Julie Ann writes:

"My testimony is just hold tight to Him and do what He says to do. I am covered by the blood of the Lamb and it's only by His strength that I will endure........ But I never wrapped my mind around a pre-tribulation message. I actually asked a pre-trib Pastor in my ignorance of how is he preparing the church....i was told not to worry because we are out of here before anything happens and then his congregation backed him up and was mad at me for asking and in my ignorance I told him what God had talked to me about preparing my family for the collapse, and to grow my food and just start to tell people of the things to come. Don't take the mark...... Oh and Paul B hits it home where he states if we deny the tribulation we deny prophecy...... :o)"

Grayson wrote:

"I sat in church a couple of years believing in Jesus but not sure of things. The church split so I did too. Seven years I walked away. I then had an overwhelming experience with the Holy Spirit in 2009. I became fearful of things to come. I couldn't get a straight answer from any pastor or believer. I began having a bible study at my home and watched the Holy Spirit begin to heal people and set people free through His people. I was searching the Word in earnest. One week before our Bible study in January of 2010 The Lord led me again into the 7 churches of Revelation and then into Matthew 24. Immediately He then led me into Thessalonians, Timothy, Jude, and Peter. He spoke to me of all the things concerning the times we live in, and assured me He was with me even unto the end of the age. I always knew I would be here, but He gave me the assurance. Especially the churches and Matthew. I looked over a congregation I was attending in the middle of 2010 and the Lord said to me,"All seven churches are here in this one gathering."

You can at least see 3-4 churches present within the walls of every assembly."

Diana said:

"I actually believed in my heart that I would be going through the Tribulation from the beginning of my salvation in 1980. I was not sure exactly when the Lord would take us out. I tried believing in the Pre Tribulation doctrine because that is what all the Pastors were preaching, but it left me with too many questions the Pastors could never answer. When they would try to answer one question it conflicted with other verses. One day there was a man from our church that was working at our home in January, 2011. We were commenting on all the fish, bird and animal deaths that were happening. I made the comment that I thought we were in the tribulation. He quickly said that it was impossible, because the 7 Year Peace Covenant had not been signed yet. I started Face Booking and befriended Paul Bortolazzo. He wrote about how the signing of the Peace Covenant would initiate the 70th week and that was the beginning of a beautiful ministry working with Paul along with my husband Rich. At first realizing that we would be going through the worst Tribulation that the world has ever known frightened me horribly. Oh, I would pray all the time for the Peace that Passeth all Understanding and I would get it. But one night the Lord woke me up and told me we were actually a blessed generation. He showed me a glimpse of Eternity. How any trouble we would go through is nothing compared to the Glory of being with Him forever. He spoke to my heart to share with others to research all His Promises and that it is impossible for Him to break a promise. We are to drink them in and believe. He will be walking with us as we walk through the Shadow of Death. We are not to fear, but trust Him. Since Paul started our special Site on Face Book called Antichrist Then The Rapture, I watched all of us come from fear and wanting to hide to joy and accepting and being willing to lay down our lives. This belief has caused us all to get closer to the Lord more than we have ever been in our lives. As I watch the worldly lives of the Pre Tribbers, how they are wrapped up in the World's trappings, it becomes clear by their fruit, whose beliefs in End Time Teaching is correct. The hardest part is being rejected by the ones we love and knowing their fate, if they continue in the Pre Tribulation lie. The Lake of Fire is forever and ever!"

Marsha writes:

"After I accepted the LORD at 9 years old I cant remember who told me but I remember standing in the living room and my mom was on the couch. I ran in from outside a little upset and I asked my mom, "Mom someone (cant remember the name) told me that the world was going to end! She said Everyone knows that honey yes it is. I heard the HOLY SPIRIT speak to me, It's going to happen in your lifetime. In 08 I was laying in bed talking the LORD telling him how much to serve HIM but didn't know in what capacity. I heard a voice You serve in my TEMPLE! I said I am oh my gosh.. I wasn't sure what that meant but in Revelations 17 and 21 talks about the overcomers.. and how they would rule the nations with HIM and be Pillar in his sanctuary and one other reward for standing firm not loving their life unto death. When I saw that I knew what the RUACH HA

KODESH meant when HE whispered that to me." (Ruach Ha Kodesh - Hebrew for Holy Spirit)

Diana contributed another interesting point:

It can be frustrating at time serving the Lord. When I think of how they came against the Lord or the Apostles or the Prophets, I see a pattern. It wasn't the people outside of the knowledge of God. It was the children of Israel that gave the grief and even murdered the Prophets and came against Jesus. The same spirit prevails in the church, with hate and accusing venom in their heart, if they don't repent will be in the Falling Away. I have to ask a Pre Tribber why they work so hard preaching to the "Saved" their Pre Tribulation belief. After all, they have to agree, we are saved by Grace and if they were right, we'd be raptured right along with them. So why waste their breathe arguing? What's the point? There is a reason we try and show them our belief and that is to prepare them to not accept the Mark of the Beast. To show them that this False Teaching of Pre Tribulation Rapture has a curse of damnation with it, because at the end of the Book of Revelation is tells us if anything is added to or taken away from the words of this Prophecy, that all the curses written in this book will be given to that person. It is a matter of Salvation! As they preach against the Truth it is more than "whatever pans out". We are not allowed to change anything concerning the Prophecy. So, we do have a mission and it is unbelievably important! We are to warn those saints when we see them going in a way that can lead to death. If this causes my death in the attempt to save the brethren's lives, so be it. My life is but a vapor!

I pray that these testimonies have encouraged you. Sometimes it is simply not enough to listen to a teacher or preacher, or even read a book. Sometimes you need to hear a word from ordinary people. This is why the Spirit prompted me to include these letters.

The Key Is Now In Your Hand

By Randy Orris

"Will there be Tribulation Saints?" Yes.

Revelation 7:13-15, *"And one of the elders answered, saying unto me, What are these which are arrayed in white robes? and whence came they? And I said unto him, Sir, thou knowest. And he said to me, These are they which came out of great tribulation, and have washed their robes, and made them white in the blood of the Lamb. Therefore are they before the throne of God, and serve him day and night in his temple: and he that sitteth on the throne shall dwell among them."*

"Will there be Tribulation Saints who will be overcome by the Beast?" Yes.

Revelation 13:7, *"And it was given unto him (the Beast) to make war with the saints, and to overcome them: and power was given him over all kindreds, and tongues, and nations. And all that dwell upon the earth shall worship him, whose names are not written in the book of life of the Lamb slain from the foundation of the world."*

All those who are overcome by the Beast by worshipping him and his image, taking the mark of the Beast, and the number of his name, will be blotted out of the Book of Life for eternity. In Revelation 3;5 Jesus Christ said, *"He that overcometh, the same shall be clothed in white raiment; and I will not blot out his name out of the book of life, but I will confess his name before my Father, and before His angels."*

God can and will remove the names of everyone from the Book of Life who take the Mark of the Beast and those who intentionally change God's words:
 (Rev. 22:18-19)

"For I testify unto every man that heareth the words of the prophecy of this book, If any man shall add unto these things, God shall add unto him the plagues that are written in this book: And if any man shall take away from the words of the book of this prophecy, God shall take away his part out of the book of life, and out of the holy city, and from the things which are written in this book."

"Will there be Tribulations Saints who will overcome the Beast?" Yes. Revelation 15: 2, *"And I saw as it were a sea of glass mingled with fire: and them that had gotten the victory over the beast, and over his image, and over his mark, and over the number of his name, stand on the sea of glass, having the harps of God."* Luke 10:20, *"Notwithstanding in this rejoice not, that the spirits are subject unto you; but rather rejoice, because your names are written in Heaven."*

The Key to overcoming is the confession of and the application of the Blood of the Lamb!

"The blood of Jesus Christ his Son cleanseth us from all sin" when *"we walk in the light, as he is in the light."* By walking in the light we also have fellowship with one another." I John 1:7

If you are reading these words during the Great Tribulation say **"No"** to the Beast, do not worship him or receive his mark. Say **"Yes"** to the Lord Jesus Christ by finding shelter in His blood, by boldly proclaiming the word of your testimony, and do not love your life unto the death. Revelation 12:11 was written just for this specific moment that you are now experiencing.

The Prophet Daniel Gets the Last Word

The Prophet Daniel, writing from the city of ancient Babylon, was the prophet that Jesus Christ quoted in Matthew 24 :15 when He said that we would *"see"* the ABOMINATION OF DESOLATION standing in the Holy Place. (Daniel 9:27).

The Prophet Daniel also saw the ultimate triumph of the Lamb and His faithful saints
over the one who is called Lucifer, Satan, the Devil, the Dragon, the Beast, the Man of
Sin:

"And he (the Antichrist) shall speak great words against the Most High, and shall wear out the saints of the Most High, and think to change times and laws: and they shall be given into his hand until a time and times and the dividing of time. But the judgment shall sit, and they shall take away his dominion, to consume and to destroy it unto the end. And the Kingdom and Dominion, and the greatness of the Kingdom under the whole Heaven, shall be given to the people of the saints of the Most High, whose Kingdom is an everlasting Kingdom, and all dominions shall serve and obey Him."
Daniel 7:25-27

Final Thoughts

I never thought that I would write a book such as this. The urgency that I felt to get this to publishing was strong. At every hand I watched as God provided. I never have written anything in this short of a period of time that involved so much. So many things 'fell into place' as I was writing. My friend Paul Bortolazzo graciously offered to allow me to quote his book Til Eternity, which was a huge blessing. Then the testimonies flooded in to write the chapter Let Me Tell You. I asked Pastor Randy Orris to write the foreword for me. He had no idea that I was struggling with how to end the book. I had no final chapter! Then an email a few weeks ago I received had several pages from Randy that he had spent an entire day writing. I as read the text I almost jumped for joy! God had inspired Randy to write exactly what was needed! He had included a note with the text saying that if I needed what he had written to feel free to use it. Little did he know how big a thing this was.

I wrote this book for all the saints who will come to the truth of the 6th seal rapture after the Pre-Tribulation rapture is proven to be false.

I wrote this book for those who are seeking truth even now and want to be ready.

I also wrote this book to serve as a 'troubleshooting' manual for those that God is calling to be watchmen.

I wrote this book for my family, and your family. For my loved ones and yours too. Use it and help them all to understand the truth. What is that truth? That if you are alive and remain until the 7oth week of Daniel, you will have to endure persecution like you never thought. But the biggest truth is that God will be there with you the whole time!

Blessings on your journey.

Mike

Suggested Reading

Walking Backwards: The Process Of Unlearning is my first published book and deals with my own struggle to purify my life from Church traditions that were not of God. In this life we all need to closely examine why we believe what we believe and if it is not of God, kick it to the curb and walk on with Christ. Available at Amazon.com in paperback and Kindle. Also available at Barnes and Nobles in Nook format.

Bugout is the short story that is the beginning for this book. I released it on Kindle and Nook both for lovers of Christian Fiction.

Suggested Reading on Eschatology

Til Eternity by Paul Bortolazzo

The Coming, A Last Days Trilogy by Paul Bortolazzo

You will note that in Tribulation Saints, that Paul graciously allowed me to use excerpts from Til Eternity. I consider Til Eternity to be the most exhaustive primer on the Last Week of Daniel's Prophecy of 70 weeks.

Further Suggested Reading

The Barbarian Way by Erwin McManus

Radical by David Platt

A Tale of Three Kings by Gene Edwards

All of these books are available on Amazon as well as Barnes & Noble.

About The Authors

Michael Saunders: My journey with Christ began in 1976 when God so richly saved me – from myself. I have served in various local Churches in many capacities from prison minister to pastor. In the summer of 2004, God led Vicki and I to Ukraine on our first missions trip. In 2005 we birthed LTCM (Love The Children Ministries) and now serve orphans and widows in Ukraine, Mexico and at home. 2011 saw us, along with other families, birthing BHC (Bethany Home Church). In 2011 I published my first book, Walking Backwards and continue to write as God directs. Vicki and I live in Wetumpka, Alabama.

Randy Orris: Journalist, publisher and pastor, was born in Akron, Ohio. He was regenerated with the Life of God when he was 16. After graduating from High School, he was accepted in the School of Journalism at Kent State University, but instead enrolled in Bible College, and began pastoring his first church in Barberton, Ohio at the age of 19. He received his Degree in Theology from the

California Graduate School of Theology. For 42 years he has pastored churches in Ohio, Missouri, Nevada and California. His field of study includes the Aramaic background of the New Testament (the native language of Jesus); emphasizing Christ as "the believer's Indwelling Lord," and equipping the saints to be ready to stand before the Son of Man. He lives with his wife Avinell and family in Avondale, Arizona.

Contacting Michael can be done via email at no1likhim@yahoo.com.

Also visit:

Love The Children Ministries

www.ltcm.wordpress.com

Bethany Publishing

www.bethanypublishing.wordpress.com

Made in the USA
Lexington, KY
02 November 2011